To Fletcher M. Fish Wiley,

A great American from

the USAFA Class of

1965, from Harold R.

"Hal" Winton, USMA

1964.

With all best wishes,

Hal

The West Point

Class of 1964

Proudly Presents

"Fallen Warriors," written by our Classmate John F. Murray

to the

Class of 2014, our Fifty Year Affiliation Class

on the occasion of your Graduation from West Point in May 2014.

This book is a tribute to our twenty-four classmates who paid the ultimate price to defend our freedom within seven short years of our graduation.

Many of our classmates have proudly worked with the Class of 2014 over the past four years. We welcomed you to West Point in June of 2010. We marched with you back to West Point after Plebe Summer and continued to share our professional and life experiences with you throughout your four years at West Point. We have watched you grow as leaders of character and are extremely proud to be associated with your class.

The Class of 1964 is honored to share these short vignettes of our "Class Heroes" with a hope that you will help us preserve their stories and memories. We welcome and challenge you to follow in the footsteps of "The Long Gray Line" and to forever remember those hallowed words of "Duty, Honor, Country."

John F. Murray
Colonel, USA (Ret)
Author

Daniel M. Evans
Colonel, USA (Ret)
Class Chairman

Fallen Warriors

West Point's Class of 1964

Fallen Warriors

WEST POINT'S CLASS OF 1964

John F. Murray

RTP

Research Triangle Publishing

Published by
Research Triangle Publishing, Inc.
PO Box 1223
Fuquay-Varina, NC 27526

ISBN 1-884570-45-3

Grateful acknowledgment is made to the following for permission to
reprint material from the following sources:

The article "I'm sorry, Sargeant, The Lieutenant Is Dead," from the
Pentagram News.

The article "' Nothing is News' when he died, but now a pilot is remembered," by Steve Marantz. Reprinted courtesy of The Boston Globe.

The paragraphs following the photographs of each Fallen Warrior are
quoted with permission from the *Howitzer*, the West Point annual for
1964.

Cover Design by Micah Sanger

Library of Congress Catalog Card Number: 96-67866

Printed in the United States of America
10 9 8 7 6 5 4 3 2 1

Contents

ACKNOWLEDGMENTS

Many people made significant contributions to this book. They are as follows and I heartily thank each of them:

Howie Bachman
Dario Baratto
David Baratto
Evelyn Batson
Anne Black
Larry Brewer
Jed Brown
Jack Bujalski
Rita Caldararo
Richard Carr
Al Carver
Richard Chilcoat
Al Christensen
Al Conetto
Cris Crissman
Walter Daniel
Chuck Davis
Richard Dexter
Carl Dye
R. E. Elmore

Pete Elson
Bruce Foster
Waldo Freeman
Ralph Galloway
Norman Gill
Pat Graves
Martin L. Green
Bob Gregson
Jack Grubbs
Nancy Hansen
Jim Harding
William Harris
John Holland
Linda Hottell
Seth Hudgins
Dorothy Hutchison
Vicki Hutchison
Paul Inwright
Bill Jackman
Adelaide Kaufman

i

Kevin Kelley
Art Kelly
Thomas W. Kelly
Chet Kempinski
Tom Kerns
Eileen Kiley
Kevin Kiley
Jim Kindleberger
Geoffrey Kleb
Sam Lamback
Linda Law
Linda Lindsay
Geoffrey Louis
Ann Palma McAbee
Barry McCaffrey
Mike McKinley
Dan McKittrick
Jack McKittrick
Marty Michlik
Mike Moran
Bill Murdy
John W. Murray
Louise Murray
Marisa Murray
Michele Murray
Marilyn Nawrosky
Dick Nowak
Roger H. Nye

Nancy Pocock
Fred Pope
Jeanne and Brendan Quann
Charles Ramsay
Robert Ramsay
Paul Rennie
Ann Reynolds
Karl Robinson
Woods Rogers
J. W. Ryan
Pauline Scholton
Janette and Bob Serio
John Shaner
Mike Sierra
Betty W. Smith
Annette and Cris Stone
Sallie Stone
Linton T. Stroud
R. Terry Thompson
Kenneth Tirella
Edward Wallin
Elizabeth and Paul Walters
John Ward
Huba Wass de Czege
Sig Weiner
Steve Weisel
Mike Willingham
Dan Winter
David M. Zeckser

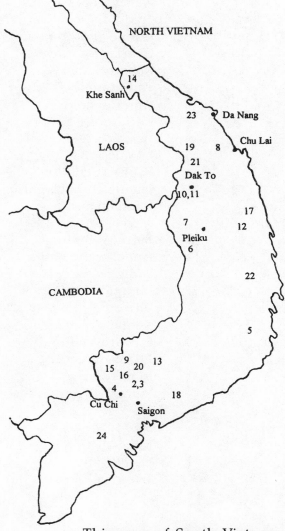

This map of South Vietnam indicates, by chapter number, the approximate locations of where the warriors of the Class of '64 fell in combat.

INTRODUCTION

Over 58,000 names of American servicemen and women are inscribed on "The Wall," the Vietnam Memorial in Washington, D. C., as a tribute to them for making the ultimate sacrifice. Each of them was following orders while serving their country in an unpopular conflict that dragged on for over a decade. Their numbers represent both sexes, practically all races and religions, and a great variety of cultural and educational backgrounds. Although the age spread was substantial, most were in their early twenties, surely awaiting long, fulfilling lives ahead. In addition, approximately 300,000 Americans were wounded in Vietnam (153,303 were wounded seriously enough to be hospitalized). By contrast, South Vietnam's military casualties doubled those of the United States, while those of North Vietnam (including the Viet Cong) were more than ten times greater.

The purpose of this book is to pay tribute to twenty-four dedicated young warriors from the United States Military Academy (USMA) class of 1964. Twenty-three lost their lives in Vietnam, one lost his in the Dominican Republic. They were special, each in his own way—each was a true American patriot.

The twenty-three men of West Point's Class of 1964 who died in the Vietnam War also represent significant diversity in spite of all having the same Bachelor of Science Degree and being relatively close in age. Within the class they include the major religious affiliations, one African American, and one son of a former Hungarian freedom fighter. They represent sixteen different states of our nation, the most (three) being from New York. Interestingly enough, half of the victims stood in the upper half of the class, academically, and half were in the lower half. They were also equally divided along regimental lines, twelve having been in the first regiment as cadets, and twelve in the second regiment.

Also included in this book is a tribute to the first member of the Class of '64 killed in combat, Charlie Hutchison, who was a victim of the conflict in the Dominican Republic in 1965. His story is first since the chapters are arranged in chronological order according to when the men died.

This book does not attempt to plunge into the history and politics of the Vietnam War (or the Dominican Republic Conflict). Volumes have been written about the foreign policy of the United States over the course of the years, especially concerning our involvement in Vietnam. Right or wrong, since that involvement is the reason this book is being written, I feel that a short historical summary is in order.

In 1950, in an effort to prevent French Indochina from falling to Communism, the United States began to grant military aid to the French forces in Southeast Asia and opened a MAAG (Military Assistance and Advisory Group). The 1954 Geneva Accords divided Vietnam into two countries, Communist led North Vietnam, north of the Seventeenth Parallel, and South Vietnam, to the south. The French began to depart after their defeat at Dien Bien Phu in 1954 and by 1958 the North began infiltrating political cadres and military reinforcements into the South. By 1962 the infiltration was large scale and the insurgency greatly expanded. USMACV (U.S. Military Assistance Command Vietnam) was created in February and by the end of the year there were 11,000 U.S. advisors in the country.

In the spring of 1964, opinion surveys showed that more than two-thirds of the American public said they paid little or no attention to what was going on in Vietnam. In fact, on 3 June 1964, when the Secretary of the Army, Stephen Ailes, was addressing the graduating class at West Point, he only made two glancing references to Vietnam as he discussed the army's mission to support the foreign policy of the United States. President Lyndon B. Johnson wanted to keep the situation low-key, but shortly after an American destroyer was attacked by North Vietnamese patrol boats in the Tonkin Gulf in August 1964, the U.S. Senate and House of Representatives passed the Tonkin Gulf Resolution. This resolution stated in effect that the United States regarded Vietnam as vital to its national interests, to world peace, and to security in Southeast Asia. In addition, the Congress should approve and support the determination of the president to take all the necessary measures to repel any armed attack against the forces of the United States and to prevent further aggression.

By early 1965, however, the Communist North Vietnamese seemed to be getting the upper hand, so the American government decided to take stronger action in an effort to prevent a Communist takeover in the South and eventually negotiate a peace settlement. After all, the dominant theme of U.S. foreign policy at that time, and until the recent end of the Cold War, was to counter Communist expansion. So, the decision was to have U.S. military units, and those of other allies, join South Vietnam's armed forces in defending their territory. On 10 March two battalions of marines arrived in Vietnam, thus beginning an escalation that would reach its peak in 1968 with over 500,000 U.S. troops in the country. Public opinion against the war began to simmer by the end of 1965 and eventually grew to a fervent state of protest, causing President Johnson not to seek re-election and prompting his successor, Richard M. Nixon, to sign the Paris Peace Accords on 28 January 1973 and subsequently pull all American troops out of Vietnam. (By the time the last U.S. unit departed two months later, well over two million Americans had served there.) The idea was for our government to provide enough munitions and supplies so that the South Vietnamese could defend themselves, but the U.S. Congress reneged on that plan. The final result was that the North Vietnamese Army overran an "out of ammo" South in April 1975.

Now, over twenty years later, our involvement in Vietnam is still widely discussed. It is discussed perhaps even more than ever with the 1995 publication of Vietnam-era Secretary of Defense, Robert McNamara's book in which he admits that he and the other senior advisors to President Johnson were wrong in not halting the war early on, that they ignorantly blundered ahead, sustained by wishful thinking.

As stated earlier, this book will not delve into the political aspects of the Vietnam conflict, but I do feel that it is important to comment on the attitude of our military, those of us who went to war because our country asked us to go, and even more importantly, because we saw it as our duty to go. We considered it the right thing to do, and, militarily, we did it well. However, our efforts were hampered by government micromanagement. General H. Norman Schwarzkopf, in his autobiography, *It Doesn't Take a Hero*, expresses that attitude while addressing his subordinates before the 1991 Desert Storm offensive, "For the benefit of the Vietnam vets—practically the whole room—I emphasized that we're not going into this with one arm tied behind our backs." Later, after a conversation with President Bush during the "100 Hour War" he commented, "His confidence in the military's ability to do its job was so unlike what we'd seen in Vietnam that the conversation meant the world to me." Most Vietnam vets would agree with Richard Nixon's assessment that, "In the end, Vietnam was lost on the political front in the United States, not on the battlefield in Southeast Asia." I, personally, compare it to a boxer who, having won all the rounds in the fight, throws in the towel when the last round is to begin.

The Class of 1964's motto is "Stars in Store for '64." A good many of the class have attained general officer status. Without a doubt, that number would have been greater had these twenty-four warriors not fallen. They were All-American heroes. They were among the "best and brightest" in the class and in the country, and they deserve the highest respect and recognition. We miss them greatly.

At the beginning of each chapter is a cadet picture of our fallen classmate, followed by a short paragraph. These items are reproduced from the *Howitzer*, the West Point yearbook. Some of the comments (written by close friends) are of a serious nature, while others are humorous. For example, in Chapter One, Hutch is referred to as "...one of the uglier men in our class..." That comment, written by his best friend, Tom Kerns, was completely in jest—Hutch was by no means ugly. Several cadet slang terms are also employed, such as "brown boy" (the bed-covering comforter which induced deep sleep). It must be kept in mind that these lines were concocted over three decades ago by young men of the era.

Chapter One

Charles Thomas Hutchison III

Although one of the uglier men in our class, Hutch will always be one of the more memorable characters. Everything
he ever did as a Cadet was quite unbelievable. He belongs in
one of those classes all by himself, unaffected as he is by any
environment. He will never change and somehow I think we
love him just as he is-Hutch.

The lieutenant's been hit!" screamed the soldier as he saw his platoon leader go down, felled by an enemy bullet. The victim was twenty-two-year-old Second Lieutenant Charles Thomas Hutchison III. It was 10 May 1965. The place: The Dominican Republic. Lieutenant Hutchison had volunteered to lead a patrol into rebel-held territory to neutralize a 50-caliber machine-gun position that had been harassing his unit from a cupola atop a two-story building in the capital city of Santo Domingo. He led his patrol, darting doorway to doorway, down the sidewalk towards the building with the cupola. Suddenly, one of his men was wounded and stumbled toward the curb, clutching at his wounds. The lieutenant instinctively ran through the enemy gunfire to rescue his wounded soldier. Almost immediately, he took a round in the side of the head, killing him instantly.

Less than a year earlier, Charlie, or Hutch as he was called at the academy, had still been wearing cadet gray as he counted the days until graduation on June third. Now he lay lifeless in a street in a Caribbean country, the blood soaking his combat fatigues. What was Hutch doing in the Dominican Republic?

In April 1965 the government of that country requested assistance from its allies to put down a rebel insurgency which had strong Communist connections. Repressing Communism was top priority at that time for the American government and its armed forces. The numerous units stationed in Europe lived constantly at the ready in case their Warsaw Pact adversaries decided to invade Western Europe. The American response to the Communist insurgency in Southeast Asia was already beginning to expand significantly and by the end of the year 180,000 U.S. troops would be in Vietnam. Presi-

2

dent Johnson did not want another Cuba in his own backyard so, on 28 April 1965, he ordered military assistance to the Dominican Republic, mainly consisting of elements of the United States Marine Corps and the Eighty-second Airborne Division from Fort Bragg, North Carolina. The Eighty-second, the "All American" Division, was, and still is the army's most rapidly deployable division, capable of having its lead elements airborne within eighteen hours of notification. The rapid arrival of the American forces brought some levity to the Dominican Republic, where thousands of its citizens had already died. A cease-fire was signed on 30 April and peace-keeping operations were begun by the American soldiers and those of several other allied countries, thus forming the Inter-American Peacekeeping Force. For Hutch and the other participants that meant conducting patrols through the streets in order to maintain peace and eliminate pockets of resistance which seemed to be ubiquitous as there were constant violations of the peace accord. Eventually, U.S. military strength on the island reached approximately 23,000. It would take a year for the peacekeepers to completely restore stability. Hutch had been there less than two weeks, doing his part to help accomplish the mission while providing exemplary leadership for his men. He died unhesitatingly, in the service of his country, the first member of West Point's Class of 1964 to be killed in combat.

Hutch's home was Kittanning, Pennsylvania, where his father had been the county sheriff and the family actually lived in the Armstrong County courthouse complex. Throughout his early years, the sheriff's son always seemed to be in and around the courthouse offices, learning about the law and politics and making friends. His little sister, Vicki, often tagged along, and their mother, Dorothy, had the unenviable task of preparing meals for the prisoners in the county jail, right there in the same building they lived in.

Such a background gave Hutch a working knowledge of politics and a desire to someday enter the legal profession. It

3

also whetted his appetite for learning, which enabled him to stand tall in his academic endeavors at Kittanning High School. He also stood tall in the athletic world, most notably basketball, where, at six-feet-five he dominated the competition. As the team captain, Hutch led his team to the league championship and was offered nearly thirty college scholarship opportunities. In making such a tough decision, he depended heavily on the influence and ideals that had guided him throughout his youth. Advice from his parents, teachers, and friends, coupled with his own personal convictions about what would be most beneficial to him as a student, led him to the gates of West Point on 5 July 1960 to join the class of 1964.

Another Western Pennsylvania athlete who would also join the class was Altoona's Tom Kerns, who first met Hutch when their basketball teams squared off during their senior year in high school. Tom vividly remembers that trip: "One thing was very clear. Their success centered on their big man, Hutch. Honestly, 6'5" in 1960 was BIG. ... He led the state in scoring. He had the agility of a man a foot shorter and the attitude of a driven winner. We arrived in Kittanning and very quickly became aware of the world that was Hutch's. ... He could shoot the net off a basket. Well, he was their team. He was Kittanning and they were proud of it, and so was he."

Tom continues: "During that winter, we were both being recruited by the Military Academy as well as many other well-known universities, not only in the East, but all over the country—he for basketball and I for football. Later we compared notes on this topic and discovered our thoughts, opinions, and decisions were similar. We were both from middle-class America. Without athletics, there would be no opportunity for college. College was available only for the more fortunate. We grew up in towns that survived on some particular industry and we would probably wind up dedicating our lives to that industry. It was our home and we would be part of it. But suddenly this thing called basketball and football—that

4

we were doing because we thrived on competition—was offering us the opportunity to further our education.

"Our parents were beside themselves with the thought that their sons would have the opportunity to go away to school and achieve a professional level that only a few in their communities enjoyed. This was 1960. The Korean War had ended only a few years earlier. Dwight Eisenhower, an academy graduate, was president. To our parents, the Eisenhowers, MacArthurs, Bradleys, and Van Fleets were true American heroes that in their eyes were very special...both of us saw the academy's interest in us as an opportunity we could not afford to turn down. We did things to please our parents and cause them to have pride in us. They raised us to be good, contributing Americans. This was the ultimate opportunity.

"Well, neither of us was prepared academically for the next level on the education ladder. Since we hadn't planned on having the chance to go to college, we didn't take the college boards for the first time until the spring of our senior year and we did very poorly. But we had good grades in school and we had the interest of our respective coaches at West Point. We were offered the opportunity to attend Braden's Prep School, just a few miles up the Old Storm King Highway, north of West Point.

"We attended English and math classes for eight hours a day, followed by six hours in class study halls. We weren't there to have fun. But because of a special mix of characters, led by Hutch, we had a good time. Weekends allowed enough time off for us to hitchhike or walk to the academy. Saturdays in the spring at West Point were and still are special, especially for athletics. There were numerous contests to watch and we dreamed that one day we might have the opportunity to compete. We retook the college boards in late June and achieved a score sufficient to allow us to join the Class of '64.

"Thus, the first step was taken that would allow us the honor of wearing the uniform of our country. In early July Sheriff Hutchison picked up several of us from Western Penn-

5

sylvania for the journey to West Point. Without the interstate highway system, it was an eleven-hour trip. It was the beginning of a long relationship for not only us future cadets, but also for our parents. The Kerns and Hutchisons made frequent weekend trips together and remained friends for many years."

From the first day of "Beast Barracks" (officially called New Cadet Barracks), Hutch knew he was in for a challenge. From being a "Big Man on Campus" at Kittanning High School, he was suddenly just one of over 800 new cadets at the United States Military Academy, struggling through a day like he had never had before. It seemed like there were a million things to do, all while being screamed at by upperclassmen who demanded that for the entire year every plebe must maintain a bracing position (chin thrust back, neck to the rear) whenever in the presence of upperclassmen in the cadet areas, barracks, and mess hall. Although he was exhausted at the end of the day and ordered to go to bed, like many of his classmates, Hutch did not sleep well. "What have I gotten myself into?" he wondered, and "How am I ever going to get all those socks, handkerchiefs, and underwear folded into neat little stacks in my locker?" As he finally drifted off to sleep, he imagined what it would be like as a big jock on a civilian campus.

During the summer many of the new cadets resigned, most of them realizing that military life was not to their liking. Hutch wasn't exactly enjoying himself, and, as is normal during "Beast Barracks," occasionally thought about resigning. However, as was the case with most of his classmates, he hung in there, convincing himself that things would get better. He knew how important a West Point education was and he knew he was smart enough and tough enough to muck it out and graduate in four years. But he didn't like starving! It seemed that mealtimes were spent reciting the volumes of plebe "poop" (knowledge) that each new cadet had to memorize—the "Alma Mater," the cheers, the chain of command, the "Days" (the number of days remaining until each key event during the year), the movie schedule, and on and on. Very little time was left for eating, which had to be done in tiny bites with the chin crammed in. Collectively, the Class of '64 lost several thousand pounds during the summer of 1960.

Charlie Hutchison was beginning to resemble a skeleton. Soon enough though, "Beast Barracks" was over and the academic year began—with a twenty percent heavier academic load for the new plebes. In addition to mathematics, English, foreign language, engineering fundamentals, physical education and tactics, three new courses were to be required and would be taken in succession—physical geography, world geography, and astronomy. This was the first of many changes that would befall the Class of '64 which, in the eyes of its members, would become the "experimental class." It certainly made for a highly challenging academic year for Hutch, who quickly found there was a big difference between high school and college academics, at least those at West Point. In fact, the courses seemed to get more difficult each year, but Hutch put his nose to the grindstone and did not let the academic department get the better of him. His outlet was basketball, where he was a valuable forward, first on the plebe team and later on the varsity. In his first-class (senior) year, the team put together one of its best records ever, going 19 - 7, with a victory over Navy and a third-place finish in the National Invitation Tournament.

Despite the rigors of academy life, Hutch was able to adapt to all situations and was extremely popular and well liked. He was always willing to help whenever a favor was asked of him and he rarely asked for a favor for himself. One of his high school friends, Linton Stroud, remembers when he was stationed at West Point in 1963 and 1964 as a member of the Army Band: "And while there, Charlie was a true leader of his fellow men. He had a magic of attracting people to him, and they really respected him. We lost him too soon in life. But he was admired by me and the people who had come to

7

know him very much. I played taps at his military funeral, which was the saddest day I have known."

Hutch and Tom Kerns continued their strong friendship as the two flourished on the fields of friendly strife. Tom was a mainstay on the Army line (those were the days of two-way football) as the team had winning seasons every year. Although Navy had their number, Tom and his teammates were victorious against Penn State all three of their varsity seasons. As luck would have it, the two buddies ended up being roommates during their last two years in Company L-2. Tom often tells the following story about how they chose their first duty assignment a few months before graduation: "We were required to turn in a selection slip by 10 P.M. At 15 minutes till, I asked Hutch what he was going to do. (He didn't know and neither did I.) He said, 'You know, Fort Bragg is close to Duke, NC State, and the beach. Think of having all those girls that close by!' I said, 'Sounds good to me!' He said, 'Well, hell, we might as well go Airborne, Ranger, Infantry!' Honest to God, that's how we made that decision—in two minutes at the eleventh hour, thinking of the girls in North Carolina. A little different thinking, he might not have lost his life and I might not have spent a tour in Santo Domingo and two in Vietnam trying to lose mine."

After graduation, Hutch hopped in his silver Corvette and returned home to be with his family and friends for what would be his last summer. His sister, Vicki, then in high school, enjoyed those times with her older brother, the prankster. Among her many memories is one of Hutch water-skiing down the river on a ladder! Another is when, earlier, he had let her win a swimming race (she was on the swimming team) and she was so happy. It did a lot for her self-confidence, as she didn't realize what really happened for years. Later she would remember his funeral procession: "The old veterans of the town had gathered on the corner in the park. As Charlie went by, they all stood and saluted. I can't pass that corner without seeing them honoring Charlie."

Hutch raised hell with his old buddies all summer. They all revered him and have submitted numerous anecdotes to this anthology. From Terry Thompson: "I was an 'at-risk' young man in junior high school, a poor student, running with the wrong crowd and headed the wrong direction. Charlie befriended me, for some reason he cared about me. He went out of his way to spend time with me and keep me out of trouble. He truly was my best friend.

"His car—or Thomas C.'s (as his father was affectionately referred to) station wagon. It was filled with basketballs, sweatshirts, cups, papers, and anything else Charlie discarded. He would pull the front seat clear back to leave room for his long legs and away we would go to our next game. If we needed something to eat, chances were we could find something in the car.

"I remember the boat trips on the Allegheny, the family's camp in East Brady. How his relatives got together and enjoyed life and each other! How kind they always were to me!"

Doctor John M. Shaner, a superintendent of schools at this writing, sent the following: "We grew up together and shared so many of life's great experiences, and I will always think of him as my brother. I believe it was Benjamin Franklin who once said, 'A brother may not always be a friend, but a friend will always be a brother.'

"Although he had great academic potential, studies took a backseat to good times and basketball. He was first and foremost a team player and he was a vicious competitor. We beat our arch rival twice during our championship senior year, and Hutch won both games in the closing seconds with his 'soft jumper' from the top of the key.

"One time we crawled among the high beams above the gym ceiling in our school just to paint our names on the steel beams. Twenty years later I was the principal of the school and I crawled back up there and found the names still there.

"When Hutch was a plebe and I was a freshman at Penn State, Army came to State College to play basketball. Hutch came to the men's clothing store where I worked and insisted that I sell him some civilian clothes. After a protest, I did so, and he put them on. When he went outside, he ran straight into a colonel who admonished him and sent him back in the store to replace the clothes with his uniform. Hutch told me to bring them to him later when we were to meet outside the hotel after bed check. I did so, he put them on again, and off we went to the fraternity parties. We returned, a bit under the weather, just as the team bus was loading to depart. The colonel immediately took charge of Hutch and sent me on my way. Hutch later told me that the hours he spent walking the area were well worth the time we had.

"When Charlie died, an army sergeant accompanied his body home and remained with the casket throughout the days of viewing and the funeral. The evening of the first day, after the last mourners had left, I invited him to accompany myself and several of Charlie's close friends to a little bar to have something to eat and a few beers. After a little encouragement he finally agreed to accompany us. He did so each night he was there and would sit and listen as we all told stories of our exploits with Hutch. I believe he really came to know the kind of guy Hutch was and how much he was loved. He always maintained his military bearing until the moment came at the funeral when he presented the flag to the parents. At that time all the emotion came to the surface and he began to cry. He stepped back and saluted and then came to stand with us, Charlie's friends. He cried along with us as if he had known Charlie as we had. We saw him off when he left town and I don't think any of us have ever forgotten him or his kindness. I feel sure he has never forgotten those days either. Even in death Charlie made a new friend."

In August Hutch reported to Fort Benning, Georgia, for Airborne and Ranger training, which he completed successfully before joining the Eighty-second Airborne Division's First Battalion, 325th Infantry. He spent his first few months on the post basketball team and was just getting broken in as an airborne infantry platoon leader when the alert order sent him and his men to the Dominican Republic. Shortly thereafter Hutch requested permission to remove the machine-gun nest. In making that request, he unknowingly committed to death as fully as he had committed himself to life. In completing his mission, Hutch gave his life for his country and for his men. No greater sacrifice can be made by any man.

A few hours later, a few miles away, Tom Kerns got the bad news. He recalls: "I know today that I immediately went into shock. How could it happen? How could a person so young—with so much to offer—with so little experience—whom I had relied on over the past four years to help me maintain my wits—be sacrificed in such a way? We had a life to live together; we were just beginning. We had both struggled together to survive four years at West Point and had finally graduated. We completed Airborne and Ranger Schools together, and together we elected to be assigned to the "All American" Eighty-second Airborne Division at Fort Bragg. How could it be? We had rejoiced together that previous spring when it became obvious that there was a war coming. After all, General Eisenhower spent all those years as a captain in a peacetime army. A war was coming for us! We were anxious. We were confident. We had completed four years at West Point, the absolute best preparation for combat in the history of warfare. But all of a sudden, it was about the loss of a buddy. I missed that preparation. It wasn't supposed to be like this.

"I recognized back then, and feel the same today—I dearly loved the guy. I was closer to him than either of my brothers or anyone I've met since. And yet he wasn't a sentimental person, nor was I. It was his attitude that drew you to him. He wasn't really a very good cadet (nor was I) but he was very intelligent. I can vouch for that—he spent many hours helping me get through. He was a tremendous athlete, and not just in basketball. He physically excelled in anything, whether on the field of play or in the field. And he knew no fear. ..."

Janet and Tom Kerns named one of their sons Hutch. Amazingly, he is very much like his namesake, much to the joy of his parents.

To those of us who knew and loved Charlie Hutchison, his passing does not dim our memory of him. He was a man's man and he lived a man's life. To him, life itself was an obsession to which he was dedicated, and his every moment was crowded with a sincere interest in the people and things which surrounded him. Hutch is sorely missed by his family, friends, and classmates, but he will never be forgotten.

Chapter Two

Clair Hall Thurston, Jr.

Having come from an Army family, Clair came to West Point with a deep inner motivation. His efficiency, determination and conscientious nature, combined with his well-known smirk, have kept him reaching for the top throughout his Cadet career and made us all proud to be associated with him.

Clair Thurston and his several classmates in the 173d
Airborne Brigade had just arrived in Vietnam when
they got word of Charlie Hutchison's death in the Dominican Republic, half a world away. The news was shock-
ing in itself, but it also served to heighten their awareness of
their own vulnerability now that they too were in a combat
zone. Even so, not one of them could have imagined that in
less than six months Clair and David Ugland (Chapter 3)
would become the Class of '64's second and third fallen warriors.

On 5 May 1965 the "Sky Soldiers" of the 173d began arriving at the Bien Hoa Air Base as it became the first major
U.S. Army combat unit to fight in Vietnam. Its mission was to
defend the vital complex of bases around Saigon. The brigade did so by clearing threatening areas in the vicinity and
within four months it had also penetrated War Zone D (north
of Bien Hoa) three times and flown to the Central Highlands
for operations.

The "Sky Soldiers" began Operation Hump (so named
because the troops had just gone over the hump—the halfway point of their one-year tour of duty in Vietnam) in the
dangerous "Iron Triangle" area on 5 November. On 8 November the First Battalion, 503d Infantry engaged a regiment of
NVA (North Vietnamese Army) in what was to be the heavi-
est fighting of the war up to that time. It was later identified
as the Q-761 Regiment and was estimated to be four to five
times the strength of the 1/503d that fought it.

It wasn't long before B Company was pinned down by
heavy enemy fire from its left flank. Second Lieutenant Clair
Thurston, one of the company's platoon leaders, volunteered
to lead his platoon around the flank of the hostile machine

14

guns with the objective of seizing a key hill. Even though he was only twenty-two years old, he had already experienced almost six months of combat with the 173d Airborne Brigade's search and destroy operations and had been wounded by grenade fragments just a month before. His only thought that day, 8 November 1965, was to inspire his troops to accomplish the mission. Leading his men in the attack, Clair took pains to maintain his own position between his soldiers and the enemy at all times. When all was ready, he rose and gave the classic infantry order, "FOLLOW ME!" and led the assault on the hill. Just thirty feet from his objective, he came under direct enemy fire, was hit, and died instantly. For his actions he was posthumously awarded the Distinguished Service Cross, our nation's second highest combat medal. Clair's other decorations include the Purple Heart with Oak Leaf Cluster, the Combat Infantryman's Badge, and several Vietnamese service and campaign awards. John "Dutch" Holland, one of the men on the ground with Clair that fateful day later said, "Lt. Thurston was very respected by all the enlisted paratroopers and proved to be a real man when it was required. He was very baby-faced and non-physical looking but in my memory he was as brave a man as I've ever met!"

Word of Clair's death quickly spread throughout the battalion area. Bob Gregson, who was wounded in the same battle, was devastated when he heard the bad news. He and Clair were like brothers, having gone through "Beast Barracks" together and later being cadet roommates. They even had shared a house together on Okinawa.

Somewhat later, the following article, "I'm Sorry, Sergeant, the Lieutenant Is Dead," by Sergeant J. W. Ryan, was published in *The Pentagram News*:

The operator answered, "Bravo switch, Sir."
"Let me speak to Lieutenant Thurston please. ..."

"I'm sorry, sir. . . Lieutenant Thurston is dead. ..."

In this way I learned of the death of Clair H. Thurston, 2d Lieutenant, Infantry, 173d Airborne Brigade. The first time I met Lieutenant Thurston I was lying very close to the ground on a landing zone just south of the Dong Nai River as Viet Cong snipers took pot shots at his platoon. It was the first enemy fire I had experienced and it seemed as though every shot was directed at me. He was running in a low crouch from man to man checking his platoon and was startled to see my unfamiliar face. "Who are you?" he inquired.

"Brigade PIO, Sir, I'm going to record what I can of this operation." I indicated a portable tape recorder and the microphone attached to my pack suspenders.

He grinned and shook his head, "O.K., glad to have you along." During the next three days, I followed him. I recorded the briefings he gave his squad leaders, and bit by bit I remembered the things I had learned as an infantryman several years before, but had little use for them as a writer in the information office.

We hacked through the dense jungle and for one stretch we never saw the sky for twelve hours. When the operation was over and we emerged from the darkness of the forest into the blinding sunlight of the landing zone he checked to ensure that every man had all his equipment. He came up to me and apologized for not being able to give me more time and suggested that I drop in at his company and chat further with him. Then he indicated an incom-

16

ing flight of extraction helicopters and told me not to miss my ride.

Months passed and the next time I saw him he was the one lying very close to the ground. The back of his trousers had been cut away and a medic was dressing his buttocks and the back of his leg that had been literally peppered with shrapnel.

He remembered me and we joked about the first time we had met and he confided that he had been as worried as I had when the shooting started. We had both seen considerable enemy fire in the months that separated the two meetings. He explained his present position by telling me how clumsy he had been in tripping a booby trap.

"Well," he quipped, "At least I'll have a chance to sit around for a while and recuperate." Then he winced as the medic applied bandages, "No, I guess I won't sit after all," he chuckled and the medics picked up a stretcher and began to carry him to a waiting medical evacuation helicopter. "Nice to see you again, Sergeant," he called back from his awkward position on the litter.

I never saw him again after that. He was a young man, four years younger than I. Younger even than my kid brother who always seemed to be of another generation. Age is a peculiar thing in Vietnam, however, it can be measured from the instant you hear the first hostile shot fired. In that respect, Lieutenant Thurston and I were the same age.

As soldiers, we were born at the same time on a landing zone a few miles across the river from War Zone D in Vietnam. He died on the

17

other side of the river, charging a Viet Cong machine gun position. He would be glad to know that 394 Viet Cong died that day opposing his battalion.

I am proud to have known him.

Clair Thurston died as he lived, a soldier's soldier. He and David Ugland were two of fifty "Sky Soldiers" slain during that day's furious battle that also left eighty-two wounded. The enemy Q-761 Regiment left almost 400 of its men on the battlefield. Losing two of its finest on the same day was a severe blow for West Point's Class of 1964. The next time such a double tragedy would occur would be a little over two years later when Mike Kiley and Hal Kaufman (Chapters 10 and 11) would perish, also while serving with the 173d. Clair Thurston was interred with full military honors at the West Point Cemetery on 10 November 1965, the first Vietnam casualty of his class to be buried in Section Thirty-four of the cemetery, an area that would later become heavily populated with other victims of that conflict.

It is said that there is nothing more devastating for parents than the loss of a child. Needless to say, it is all the worse when the young victim is the parents' only child. Such was the heartbreak of Clair's parents, Colonel Clair H. Thurston (who later would become a major general, U.S. Army Reserve, and the adjutant general of the state of Maine) and his wife, Agnes. They were as proud of their son as parents could be, for Clair, Jr., excelled in everything he ever did. Born in Lampasas, Texas, on 20 June 1943, Clair was to attend schools in Texas, Virginia, New York, Georgia, Pennsylvania, and Germany as the army moved his father around. He achieved outstanding scholastic results in all of them and in 1960 he graduated at the top of his class from the American High School in Heidelberg, Germany, receiving the Bausch and Lomb award for scientific excellence and the Heidelberg American Women's Club award for outstanding achievement.

Since his earliest childhood Clair had been determined to follow a military career so he also devoted a lot of time to his physical development and athletic prowess in order to be a well-rounded candidate for the United States Military Academy. His lofty credentials led to several scholarship offers to civilian colleges which he turned down in favor of an appointment to West Point from Senator Margaret Chase Smith from his parents' home state of Maine. He had also won a presidential appointment which he did not accept so that it could be used by someone else.

Despite his youth (he had just turned seventeen two weeks prior to arrival), Clair made a rapid adjustment to the demands of the academy. He was in the same "Beast Barracks" squad as David Ugland (Chapter 3), Dee Stone (Chapter 6), Larry Brewer, and Bob Gregson. In talking about Clair, Larry has said, "He was super! You wouldn't have known that he was the youngest in the squad because he was so serious, dedicated to perfection and mature beyond his years. We all looked up to him. Clair had a tremendous sense of vision and a winning personality."

After that first summer, the new cadets were split up and sent to the twenty-four different cadet companies at the time (The Corps of Cadets expanded to thirty-six companies after the authorized strength of the corps was increased from 2,529 to 4,417 in late 1964). These "permanent" company assignments were to last until graduation but there was another experiment in store for '64. In the spring of 1962 it was announced that each member of the class would be reassigned to another company within the same regiment. This news was not received very well at first because of various established roots such as friendships, roommates, intramural teams, company allegiance, etc. However, the mandate was carried out and at the end of the summer the new "cows" (juniors) begrudgingly reported to their new companies, generally expecting the worst. However, some pleasant surprises were encountered, and in the long run, the company changing pre-

19

sented the opportunity to know more people in one's class and in other classes. In Clair Thurston's case, he was assigned to Company H-1, where he was reunited with old "Beast Barracks" pals, Dee Stone, Bob Gregson, and Larry Brewer. "It was great to be with Clair, Dee, and Bob again after two years of little contact," remembered Larry. "Clair was more squared away than ever, excelling in all areas. He was at the top level, academically, but he always had time to help others with their studies. He was truly dedicated to his fellow man and his country."

Clair participated in numerous extracurricular activities to include the Rugby Club, where he got to know Bob Serio, another outstanding scholar-athlete who would also become a Vietnam casualty (Chapter 13). Graduating twenty-second of 565 in the class, Clair won the General Pershing Award for ranking first in the class in tactics, and the American Bar Association Award for ranking first in law.

Standing as high as he did in the graduation order of merit, Clair had his full choice of branches and probably could have gone directly into graduate study in some scholarship program. But his strong sense of duty prevailed and he chose the Infantry Branch. Although the insurgency in Vietnam was relatively low-level at that time, Clair sensed that conflict was imminent and requested assignment to the Far East. After earning his airborne wings and ranger tab, he became engaged to Miss Virginia Baumgartner of Ballston Spa, New York, in November 1964, and joined the 173d Airborne Brigade in Okinawa a month later. Clair enjoyed his short stay on the island and took advantage of the opportunity to get to know better his several classmates in the unit. They, in turn, were impressed with him, especially with the outstanding speech he gave as the youngest graduate at the annual West Point Founders Day Dinner. To this day, Jack Grubbs can recall in detail what was said by his young, but wise and mature classmate.

In May 1965 Clair arrived in Vietnam, anxious to serve his country and assist a friendly nation in its fight against Communism. In one of his last letters to his father Clair wrote: "Isn't it strange how we are willing to fight or even die for that little bit of red, white and blue bunting and Marian Anderson singing in 'The Star Spangled Banner,' 'O, thus be it ever when free men shall stand!' "

Clair Thurston has been greatly missed by all who knew him, but especially by his classmates, who revered him; by his fiancee, who lost the chance to share her life with him; and by his parents, for whom he was everything.

Chapter Three

David Leonard Ugland

Problems, problems and more problems seem to have worried everyone except "Ugie", thru his four years at the Academy. A bad first year was finished with a good last one. Minnesota should be proud of this boy. Since Academics presented few problems, the brown boy was second to none. His only parting words are -- "What me worry?" and "World, here I come."

Moments after Companies B and C of the First Battalion, 503d Infantry, had run into the enemy buzz saw that killed Clair Thurston, Company A, which was the battalion reserve, was called into the fray. Second Lieutenant David Ugland, one of A Company's platoon leaders, had just heard about his good friend Clair's death and was in somewhat of a dazed state as he directed his platoon into the heavy combat. Besides wanting to kick the enemy's tail, he desperately wanted to avenge Clair's death. After all, Clair and David had known each other well ever since they were together as teenagers in "Beast Barracks." David's men loved him and his platoon was well prepared to meet the challenge. But it was to be another unfortunate happening as Lieutenant David Ugland, whose platoon was in the center of the battle, met a soldier's death, as described in the citation accompanying the Bronze Star with "V" (Valor) presented posthumously to his family:

> While leading his platoon through heavy concentrations of Viet Cong machine-gun fire he pinpointed a hidden machine gun. After warning his platoon, he exposed himself to the hostile fire without regard for his personal safety, engaging the enemy single-handedly. Only seconds later the Viet Cong machine-gun crew recovered from the initial attack of Lieutenant Ugland and a burst of fire killed him instantly. Through his courageous actions the lead squad of the platoon had been given time to maneuver and destroy the enemy position. ...

Fellow A Company platoon leader, Al Conetto, remembers that sad event all too well: "When I reached the company area, I was told that Dave had been killed. One of his NCO's carried his body back and it lay under a poncho near the company CP. I slowly walked over, kneeled, and raised the poncho. To this day I do not recall what he looked like. I could see him alive; tall, blond, quiet, easygoing. I could not see him dead. But he was the first American soldier I saw killed in action."

David was also awarded the Purple Heart, the Combat Infantryman's Badge, and two Vietnamese medals, the Gallantry Cross with Palm and the National Order, Fifth Class. He was the second of twenty-three members of the Class of 1964 to die in Vietnam. Over 500 of the class would participate in the conflict.

David was born in Chicago on 22 April 1942. His family also lived in Toledo and Columbus, Ohio, before settling in Minneapolis, Minnesota, soon after David's tenth birthday. Throughout his early years he excelled in the classroom and in athletics. In high school he was a member of the National Honor Society, lettered in wrestling, and was chosen for the leadership position as All-School H-Y Chaplain. For several years David was a winner of the Minneapolis Star and Tribune World Affairs contest and during his senior year he won the first prize—a trip to Washington, D.C.

David first expressed a desire to attend West Point during the ninth grade when he was interviewed in connection with an award as a Minneapolis "Teen Trooper." With his sights set, he achieved outstanding results in high school and on the college boards which earned him an appointment to the Class of 1964 from Congressman Walter Judd.

As it was for most of the new cadets, "Beast Barracks" was a rude awakening for David, a daily struggle. The only ones who were semi-prepared for such physical and mental trauma were those with prior military service and those from military prep schools and military families. They had the

24

advantage of already knowing how to "spit shine" shoes, march, disassemble and clean a rifle, and countless other things a soldier must know. David even wrote home on one occasion saying that "another week of 'gigs' like the last one" would result in a trip home.

Two of the principal people responsible for transforming David and his mates into capable cadets were his squad leaders during "Beast Barracks," Cadet Corporals Clancy Matsuda (first month) and Roger Havercroft (second month) of the Class of 1962. Both proved to be rigid taskmasters who instilled in their men the necessary discipline and toughness to survive the system. They had different styles, however, with Clancy being the friendly, open type, while Roger was more distant. Unbeknownst to the eight suffering fledglings of the squad, the seemingly more distant leader had been quite impressed with their diligence and progress. Little did he know, that within only a few years, three of his young charges would become casualties of the Vietnam War. Clair Thurston and Dee Stone (Chapter 6) were the other ill-fated members of that squad. Another classmate in that squad, Larry Brewer, recounts the following story: "Several years after returning from Vietnam, while stationed at Fort Campbell, Kentucky, I ran across one of our "Beast Barracks" squad leaders, Roger Havercroft. I was surprised how happy he seemed to see me as we began chatting about the past few years. Before long, his eyes became misty as he removed from his wallet a photo of our old squad from the summer of 1960 and began commenting on the tragedy of losing three of them in combat. I have not seen Roger lately but I'll bet he still has that picture in his wallet."

David settled into life within the gray walls and proved himself equal to the challenge. Although he accumulated his fair share of demerits, he did exceptionally well in academics and won the American Legion award for standing first in the class in chemistry, one of the more difficult courses of the curriculum. He was also known for his great sense of humor

25

and his heart of gold, someone who often provided academic assistance to his less-gifted classmates.

After the challenging first two years of adjustment at West Point, David and his classmates were eagerly looking forward to the "Cow Trip" in June 1962. In the meantime, though, still another "new deal" was being concocted for the class. Until that year cadets enjoyed the tradition of beginning their third summer with a trip to various military bases around the country, sort of a gentleman's tour that was considered a carrot at the end of a rather unpleasant two-year stick. But sure enough, instead of taking the "Cow Trip" that June, the class remained on the academy grounds for a three-week course in military instruction techniques, a period which the class dubbed "New Cow Barracks" or "June Entrenchment."

But David was able to overcome that experiment as well as the other one that summer as he went from Company M-1 to Company K-1. He continued to shine in the classroom and his fine record would have qualified him for graduate training in engineering, but his goal was to work with and lead troops, so he chose infantry, the "Queen of Battle." After successfully completing the Airborne and Ranger courses, he headed for Okinawa, where he signed into the 173d Airborne Brigade in December 1964.

It was like "old home week" on the Japanese island as David was joined in the 173d by classmates Clair Thurston, Bob Gregson, Tony Hartle, Jack Grubbs, Bob Walters (Chapter 21), Larry Bryan, and Jim Koster. They had requested the assignment for a variety of reasons. One was to be part of one of the army's newest units, created in 1963 to be the elite, troubleshooting reserve in the Pacific Theatre. The 173d was some 5,000 strong at any one time and was to be the only separate airborne brigade the U.S. Army ever had. Another reason was the opportunity to jump out of airplanes and get paid for it. Airborne pay for officers was (and still is) $110 per month. That was almost half of a second lieutenant's $222.30 monthly base pay at that time. Throwing in quarters and subsistence allowance, being on airborne status meant drawing about $500 a month instead of $400. And that was before taxes!

Soon after David arrived in Okinawa, he wrote home about the brigade's intensified training in anticipation of going to Vietnam where things were beginning to heat up. And, it wasn't long before the "Sky Soldiers" were in Vietnam as the build-up of U.S. Forces got underway.

Shortly after David's arrival in Vietnam, he was stricken with one of the new strains of malaria which continued to baffle our doctors. In spite of a 104 degree fever and a loss of weight—to less than 140 pounds—six-foot-three David refused hospitalization several times. Finally, over his protests, he was evacuated to Japan in August where he regained his strength and returned to Bien Hoa in October. The return orders were difficult to obtain because he had been declared medically unfit for jungle duty, but David's determination and unit loyalty prevailed and he happily returned to his platoon in A Company of the 1/503d. Later he expressed disappointment because he had missed a skirmish just a short time before his return. He also wondered why everyone back home seemed to feel sorry for him because he was in Vietnam: "I get a kick out of these people who think I'm being a martyr or something. ... I'm glad I'm here," he wrote his parents. His last letters told of his preparations for the search and destroy mission which was to cost him his life.

When David rejoined his unit, it was in the process of conducting sweeps in the "Iron Triangle" region, thirty kilometers northwest of Saigon, until then considered inviolate enemy territory, where for more than twenty years they had been constructing a maze of tunnels, training camps, supply dumps, hospitals, schools, and rest areas. Without the clearing operations, the enemy forces in that area would pose a continuous threat to all friendly units in the vicinity of Saigon. The brigade destroyed all that it could during the October sweeps, but the enemy avoided heavy contact and the 173d and other U.S. units would have to return to the "Iron Tri-

27

angle" again and again. When the "Sky Soldiers" returned in November on Operation Hump, the enemy, enjoying superior numbers, chose to stand and fight. Casualties were high, but none were more devastating to the men of the Class of '64 than the loss of their two brave young patriots, Clair and David. Their bravery contributed significantly to the 173d's victory and its being awarded the Distinguished Unit Citation for extraordinary heroism on 8 November 1965.

David's close friends well remember the many good times at his home in Minneapolis. The Ugland house suddenly became a social center whenever David came home and the discussions usually ran far into the night, covering such a wide range of topics as politics, foreign affairs, college, the army, our futures, sports, and of course, girls. Some friends even made plans to encourage David to enter politics after his army career, but he was much more interested in a teaching career, either at the academy or at some other college. But all of these plans came to an abrupt end on that November day in a far-off jungle.

Those of us who knew David will always remember his high ideals and the many successes he achieved in just twenty-three years. His life was taken at its very peak, but the sadness of the loss is eased somewhat by the wonderful memories of the man. His parents, his older sister, his two younger brothers, and his countless friends and classmates miss him, but they also find inspiration in his memory. To them he remains much revered and never to be forgotten.

David's philosophy is expressed in the following words of the Cadet Prayer: "Encourage us in our endeavor to live above the common level of life. Make us to choose the harder right rather than the easier wrong. ..."

David Ugland was far above the "common level" and always chose the path of right, no matter how difficult it might be. Now that he is gone, those of us who remain behind salute him and only hope that we can live up to the example he provided.

Chapter Four

Harold Paul Kindleberger

K.B., a native of El Paso and the city across the river, came to West Point from the Army and poop school, with a yen for hard work, some of the time and wine, women and song, all of the time. After graduation -- Airborne, Ranger, Special Forces, all the way.

KB Kindleberger had it all. From his early youth it was obvious that he epitomized the ideal combination of leadership, intelligence, integrity, and devotion to duty. As his classmate and good friend, Carl Dye has said, "KB had GENERAL OFFICER stamped on him when he first put on a uniform." Unfortunately, though, KB was still a junior first lieutenant when he made the ultimate sacrifice, only six months after Operation Hump.

KB, or "Butch," as he was called within the family, was born on 31 October 1940 in Kalamazoo, Michigan. Sister Suzanne was already five years old and brother Jim would come along five years later. In 1948 the family moved to El Paso, Texas, where KB later attended Burgess High School, along with future West Point classmate, Al Carver. According to Al, "KB decided early in life that West Point and an army career were what he wanted. When we were in high school together, we travelled about 100 miles from El Paso in the wee hours of the morning to hunt ducks. I remember many hours of good conversation and warm companionship. On one of these hunts, KB mentioned that from the earliest days of his youth he aspired to attend West Point."

While in high school KB began to prepare for his army career. He excelled in ROTC (Reserve Officer Training Corps) and served as the battalion commander for his high school detachment. Later he was selected as the cadet colonel for all of the high school ROTC programs in El Paso. He looked the soldier; his bearing was ramrod straight. He was a fierce competitor, succeeding in all that he did. Although he wasn't the biggest or the fastest athlete in the league, he was one of the toughest and made Burgess High School history by scoring the winning touchdown in the school's first ever victory.

Shortly before graduation KB received a third alternate appointment to West Point from Senator Rutherford. That was too far down for selection, however, so he joined the Regular Army. Somewhat later he wrote to the senator again in an effort to confirm the status of his appointments. The senator confirmed that his service academy appointments were still committed and offered testing for the U.S. Naval Academy. KB complied and once again was selected as a third alternate.

Now a private first class (PFC), KB and his unit were sent to Germany by ship. After only two days in Germany, KB was notified that he was being sent to Maryland, to the Naval Academy Prep School. His army green in a sea of blue and white attracted severe harassment there. His mother recounts that KB was accepted to the Naval Academy, subject to the approval of a waiver for a slight sight problem. When so informed by a navy officer, KB replied, "No sir, never mind the waiver. I will remain a soldier." Shortly afterward, he was accepted to the U. S. Military Academy Prep School at Fort Belvoir, Virginia, (now located at Fort Monmouth, New Jersey, this school prepares qualified active-duty military personnel for acceptance to West Point) and subsequently joined the Class of 1964 on the plain at West Point in the summer of 1960. KB was one of three of the class's fallen warriors who attended the USMA Prep School. David Ramsay (Chapter 23) and John Graham (Chapter 24) were the other two.

West Point was the ideal place for KB; it was what he had prepared for and he quickly distinguished himself as a natural leader. He was a dean's-list student and a member of several clubs, including the Parachute Club, where he became good friends with Hal Kaufman (Chapter 11), Martin Green (Chapter 19), Bob Walters (Chapter 21), and John Graham (Chapter 24), who would also meet their fates in Vietnam. By the time he became a first classman (firstie), KB had so impressed his peers and superiors that he was selected to be the commander of the Second Regiment, one of only three men in the class to wear six stripes.

I remember him as a firstie. KB was a cut above, more dedicated than the rest of us. One rainy weekend when we were sitting around reading contemporary novels, I asked him what he was reading and he showed me the cover. His book was *Night Drop*, the story of an airborne operation of the Second World War. KB was also a strong admirer of General Douglas MacArthur and read all he could about him. He was thrilled to meet MacArthur that year and later carried the general's flag at his funeral.

Another new experiment for the Class of '64 brought two of its fallen warriors together during firstie year. Until that year, the first-class chain of command had been permanent for the entire academic year. But in 1963 - 1964 it was decided to have three different leadership slates, except for the brigade staff and the two regimental commanders and their executive officers, who stayed in position all year. As such, KB had three different groups of his classmates filling the positions of adjutant, assistant adjutant, training officer, and supply officer. The final group, from mid-March until graduation, saw Bob Serio (Chapter 13) live across the hall from KB as the adjutant. The two worked together harmoniously as their friendship grew. Who would have ever thought that these two class leaders would perish in a far-off land only a few years later?

After graduation, KB headed west in his Corvette to visit his family and was stopped several times for speeding. On one occasion, in Arizona, the patrolman ascertained that KB had just graduated from West Point and let him continue, on the condition that he see the justice of the peace and pay his fine en route, which, of course, he did.

Before reporting to the Airborne and Ranger courses at Fort Benning, KB drove to the Marine Corps Base in El Toro, California, to visit his brother, Jim, a nineteen-year-old PFC. Their relationship had grown strong over the years, as Jim later recalled: "During our school years at home, the difference in our ages had us all going in different directions. Our common interest during those days was watching war movies on TV late at night, mostly on weekends. KB would help me talk our mom into letting me stay up, then we would walk to the local minute market for Pepsi and Clover Club barbecue potato chips, getting ready for the big night. His spot was always lying on his back in front of the TV, head propped up on his football. Funny how such small things bring back the best memories.

"Growing up in El Paso, our dad had an old 1940 or so Dodge in our backyard. I never remember it running. But Butch and I would spend many afternoons 'driving' that car around the U.S.A., kind of like an early 'Route 66'—maybe planting the seed for the Corvette he would purchase upon graduation.

"...and the time he talked me into sticking my tongue on the metal freezer door because it tasted so good—I think our sister had done the same to him.

"Our favorite pastime during the holidays was taking turns emptying the whipped cream cans in each other's mouth. We always got into trouble, but it was too good to resist!

"I went into the Marine Corps in 1963, coming home after boot camp later that year. Butch was home from West Point on leave and a little bit of rivalry existed. I thought I was pretty tough, besides being bigger than KB. I was firmly entrenched in Marine Corps doctrine. He kicked my butt all over the front yard—my mom yelling at him not to hurt me contributed to my embarrassment. He spent most of the time laughing; I spent most of the time on the ground.

"When he came to visit me in El Toro in August 1964 he offered me the use of his Corvette while he was at Fort Benning. We drove to Las Vegas, then to El Paso where I dropped him off. I headed back to El Toro, a nineteen-year-old PFC with a new Corvette and my brother's gas credit card.

"In 1965 KB was my best man when I got married. We both were in our uniforms, he, the army second lieutenant and I, the marine corporal. I was proud to stand by him.

"KB came to El Toro on the way to Travis Air Force Base en route to Vietnam. After spending a night or two with my wife and me, we drove him to Travis. The evening we arrived at Travis we decided to have a farewell drink. Standing in front of the Officers Club, both in civvies, we wouldn't have had any problem, except for the fact that he knew I was enlisted. He wouldn't break the rules. It was either right or wrong with KB. No compromises. He always kept his word. I never dreamed that I would never see him again. ... He was always there to help me. He was a homebody, a stable force. He taught me a lot."

Al Carver continues describing how well rounded KB was: "Serious as he was in tending to business, KB loved life and he knew how to enjoy it. Early one morning when he was a young private in the army, KB livened up Fourteenth Street, near Pennsylvania Avenue, in D.C., with a spirited touch football game. On another occasion, KB added some suspense and excitement to the wedding of one of his West Point classmates. KB was the best man. One of his responsibilities was to ensure that, following the reception, the newlyweds' car would be in place, ready for a quick, no fuss departure. But when the newlyweds rushed from the church after the reception, their car was nowhere to be seen. After an appropriate delay, just enough for the prank to have the intended effect, KB appeared with the car and sent the newlyweds, Joan and me, on their way."

KB's first assignment was with the 101st Airborne Division at Fort Campbell, Kentucky. Stationed there with him was fellow infantryman, Carl Dye. In fact, KB and Carl bought a trailer off post together so that they wouldn't be saddled with the post's Bachelor Officers Quarters rules. They both enjoyed the airborne duty with the 101st but there was one problem. Although one brigade (not theirs) of the 101st deployed to Vietnam in July 1965, the remainder of the division wasn't scheduled to go for awhile, and these two patriotic young officers felt they had to go to Southeast Asia as soon as possible and make their contribution. After all, that is what they had been trained for. So, they cut short their tours with the 101st and volunteered for assignment to the Twenty-fifth Infantry Division, which was in Hawaii, preparing to deploy to Vietnam.

They joined the Second Battalion, Fourteenth Infantry, trained rigorously for a short while, and embarked via ship to Vietnam in April 1966. The Twenty-fifth was part of the build-up which saw U.S. troop strength climb from 180,000 to 280,000 during 1966. Carl remembers those days: "The days on board ship were spent rather laid back by most of us, but KB was mostly with his men—exercising and just getting to know them better. In just over three months, he became the most respected platoon leader in the battalion. This became clear when, on 11 May, after only ten days in country, KB stepped on a land mine and lost both legs. Several of his men, including his platoon sergeant, died trying to get to him, all to no avail. A dustoff helicopter eventually evacuated him, but he died on the way to the hospital. I was on the radio in the S-3 tent when the incident took place. I knew what was happening, but couldn't do a thing about it except pray he'd make it. Maybe it's best some prayers aren't answered, but this is one that should have been.

"We lost a truly great man that day, and I, for one, will always feel the world a lesser place without his presence. I doubt we will ever know why some of us are chosen so early in life to pay the ultimate price for our country. We can only pray that it was necessary."

First Lieutenant Harold P. Kindleberger was a living example of the West Point motto, "Duty, Honor, Country." They were not just words with KB. They were KB.

Chapter Five

Denis Wayne Galloway

Young Denis came to New York State after half completing his college education. Immediately, he took it upon himself to introduce West Point to culture. As a "model cadet," his career was interrupted only briefly by a pledgeship in the walking society. May he be remembered as a friend of our short, four year stay.

36

L ess than six months after KB Kindleberger became the victim of a mine, Denis Galloway met a similar fate, thus becoming the fifth warrior of the Class of '64 to fall in combat. On 24 October 1966 First Lieutenant Galloway's platoon was assigned the mission of clearing a minefield, an extremely hazardous task which is one of the functions of the Corps of Engineers. As an officer, Denis could have chosen to supervise his men from outside the minefield, but instead, he opted to lead by example and share in the removal and carrying of the mines with his soldiers. As the unit was doing its job, it came under enemy fire which caused several mines to detonate. Denis was killed instantly. Most probably, some other young soldier later returned home alive because he was not holding a mine at that moment. Denis had deployed with the lead elements of the 101st Airborne Division and had only been in country for a short time. In corresponding with his old roommate, Jim Carson, he had indicated that he was thriving on the responsibility and challenge of leadership in combat. It is also interesting to note that he was the first and only member of the class to perish while serving with the 101st, the unit KB Kindleberger had left because it wasn't deploying soon enough.

Denis was from Elsberry, Missouri, where his heartland upbringing afforded him the opportunity to work hard and go to church on Sundays and learn how to sing. He was the son of Eileen and Ralph and the older brother of Diane and Nena. Denis was an outstanding scholar and athlete in high school and later attended Washington University in St. Louis for two years before entering West Point in the summer of 1960. His background, intelligence, and experience greatly facilitated his adjustment to the rigors of the academy and he

37

came to be known as "Uncle Denis." He faithfully subscribed to the *The Elsberry Democrat* and always passed it around for all to benefit from its down-home philosophy and humor. One particular notice which he cut out and saved stated, "All hunting, fishing and berry picking on the Floyd Galloway farms will cease, the privilege has been abused."

Denis was big enough to play football, but during his plebe year his singing ability qualified him for the Glee Club, so he chose that over the gridiron. Besides, the Glee Club took regular weekend trips to exciting places with refined people who invariably had daughters they wanted to introduce to a cadet.

After a successful, but uneventful two years in Company K-2, Denis was reassigned to Company M-2, a "flanker" (tall cadet) company that was considered to be the most easygoing in the corps. Until 1958 the Corps of Cadets was sized by company in order to streamline parades. For example, the first company to march onto the plain was A-1, a flanker company. Then the companies gradually got shorter, reaching their lowest point with the "runt" companies of M-1 and A-2. Finally they got taller again, ending with M-2, the other tallest company with A-1. Through the years, companies developed their own reputations along the general lines that the flanker companies were loose and the runt companies were "chicken" (strict), especially for plebes. A significant problem with the sized companies persisted within the intramural sports program in which all cadets participate (unless, of course, one is on a varsity team at the time). The size disparity made it most difficult for the runt companies when they competed against the flankers in such sports as basketball and football. By 1962 that problem was solved, but the runt and flanker complexes still lingered.

When the new cows, flanker Denis Galloway, and runt, Jim Carson, checked into Company M-2 in September 1962, they figured life was going to be great, as the casually dressed company commander greeted them with a beer in his hand.

And to make it even better, M-2 was located in the famous "lost fifties" divisions, around the corner and out of sight of North Area. No one ever came there except their own tactical officer (TAC), and his visits were somewhat predictable. For Denis it would not be that great of a change, but for Jim, it would be a 180-degree turn from his old runt company, C-2, where, as a plebe, he was once stuffed into a wall locker with three other classmates and further tormented as an upperclassman poured lighter fluid on its surface and lit it.

At first, Jim was assigned to room with Seth Hudgins, but after a short while, the TAC realized that two "goats" (low in academic standing) in the same room was not a good idea, so he designated the "hive" (high in academics), Denis, to be Jim's roommate. It is not clear whether Denis helped bring Jim's grades up, or Jim caused Denis's grades to drop, but the bottom line was that the two forged a strong friendship and both graduated on time, with Denis in the upper twenty percent of the class. However, it turned out to be a most interesting two years.

After settling into their new home, Denis and Jim began going out after taps on Friday nights. They had gotten to know some New York City girls with local Italian connections and would scramble up the hill behind the "lost fifties," jump into the girls' car, scrunch down in the backseat while passing through the Military Police (MP) gate, and proceed into the neighboring town of Highland Falls. There, they would go to Mama Gallu's and do what normal college students did: drink beer, eat pizza, and talk. Mama Gallu always put them in a private upstairs room in order to avoid the MP's who often came by on their rounds. Eventually, though, an over-zealous duty officer decided to inspect the "lost fifties" rooms after taps and the two revelers were reported for not being in their room.

In such cases, the charged cadets had to provide a written response to the TAC, which Denis and Jim did, simply stating that the report was correct, they were out of their room.

However, the West Point legal system is quite demanding and the TAC informed them, "You birds have to tell me where you were and what you were doing." At this critical juncture, the Cadet Honor Code prevailed. "A cadet will not lie, cheat, or steal, nor tolerate those who do." A lie, to the effect that they were studying in someone else's room, would have resulted in a mere eight demerits each. That was not even a thought, though, as Denis, without hesitation spilled the details. Later, at the Punishment Board, the regimental tactical officer, a colonel, said, "Too bad you got caught; forty-four, eighty-eight, and four." That meant forty-four demerits, eighty-eight hours of walking the area and four months of room confinement. Such a sentence signified the end of their legal extracurricular activities—the Track Team for Jim, and, for Denis, his beloved Glee Club. It also put an abrupt end to dating those two young ladies.

At first, Denis took the slug (punishment) hard—he hadn't been used to walking the area on Wednesday and Saturday afternoons and being confined to his room the rest of the time he wasn't in class or formation. But soon his intellect and sense of optimism about life took over and he taught Jim and some of the other "area birds" to play verbal chess while passing each other on the area. Such mental stimulation helped them greatly, because with some additional demerits they picked up, they both ended up walking the area from early November until June. In fact, they earned their way into the Century Club, a highly selective group that only accepts those who walk at least 100 hours on the area. Denis also took advantage of the extra time in his room to learn to play the guitar and read at least three novels a week.

Jim recalls the following episode of that era: "One day... Denis put me up to a trick. We had been reading a lot in confinement and read *Catch 22*. Yossarian was a fictional hero to us, always another mission to fly. So, here's what Denis thought up. Note that he also thought to tell me I didn't have

WEST POINT'S CLASS OF 1964

a hair if I didn't do it, somewhat removing himself from the risk. ... Denis was in the upper portion of the class.

"Before walking punishment tours there was an inspection in ranks. During one of those inspections, I took one of the first positions, gave my name as Yossarian, and passed inspection without any demerits. As the inspecting officer and guard passed on down the line of cadets, I did a smart two steps to the rear, left turn, and marched to the end of the line and took my place to be inspected again with my right name. (No advantage to be had, you see, even double jeopardy.) Again I passed inspection with no demerits.

"Each hour the guard called out our names, and we had to answer to show we were present. When he came to Yossarian no one answered. The guard called again and again. By the time he went to report the absence to the duty officer we were all in tears from the restrained laughter we had to endure. When the duty officer appeared and called out Yossarian, we had had enough and broke out in rolling laughter that infected the whole area squad."

When the year finally ground to a close, half of the class went to Germany for a month of Army Orientation Training (the other half had gone the year before). Denis was assigned to an engineer unit near Budigen as an acting platoon leader and third lieutenant. There he met and fell in love with Sigrid, the girl he would have married had not his life so cruelly ended. During firstie year, Denis and Sigrid wrote frequently, and he stared at her picture a lot.

In the spring of 1964 when the firsties ordered their new cars (which they were authorized to have one month before graduation—for many years now firsties have been authorized to have cars during their entire last year), Denis selected a cheap and practical mode of transportation, which to those not in the know, seemed quite strange for a bachelor. The reason was that he already had a 1958 Corvette which he had acquired brand new and maintained in the family garage back in Elsberry. It was his pride and joy which he only used when he was home.

Jim Carson continues: "I can remember him sitting at the desk in our room, playing a song by the name of 'Down in the Mines' on his guitar, or reading the *Elsberry Democrat* which became an institution for its down-to-earth editorials, grassroots wit, and vignettes of that portion of Americana which he loved. ... I remember Denis frozen in time as a handsome, courageous young lieutenant that his country, family, men in his platoon and USMA could be proud of. Like that great book on Vietnam is titled, we were soldiers once, and young."

During his brief combat tour, Denis was awarded the Silver Star, Bronze Star, Purple Heart, and two Vietnam Medals.

Denis was laid to rest in the Elsberry Cemetery, only a half mile from home. His pride and joy, the '58 Corvette, is still in perfect condition in the family garage.

Chapter Six

Dee Wayne Stone, Jr.

A product of New York's tough West Side (Tennis Club), Dee
has remained calm and unperturbed throughout his four year
sojourn despite frequent bouts with the T.D. and, occasionally, the N. Y. State Highway Patrol. His ability to come out
on top in any situation will make him a sought-after friend in
whatever strata of society he chooses to claim.

On 11 November 1966 Dee Wayne Stone, Jr., became the sixth fallen warrior of the Class of '64 and the third from that unfortunate "Beast Barracks" squad that already lost Clair Thurston and David Ugland. It seems incredible that half of the first six casualties of the class would come from the same original squad.

Perhaps one of the most symbolic episodes of Dee "Bud" Stone's short life occurred in the summer of 1960, during "Beast Barracks," when the new cadets at West Point were generally petrified, afraid to do anything that might cause a horde of upperclassmen to descend upon them screaming. Woody Rogers, one of Dee's classmates, recalls the incident as follows: "A scared plebe, I double-timed across Central Area, anxious that this short trip might end in disaster should I run into an upperclassman. Another plebe passed quickly, but I heard and sensed a sudden shoe scrape as he turned and, seemingly, began tracing my footsteps, soon breathing down my neck. Then, to my amazement, I heard, 'Pssst. Hey, Rogers, follow me.' Who was this crazy guy speaking out loud to me in such a location? I followed him up the stoops of some foreign division neither of us knew, and into some classmate's room, equally unknown. The big fellow said, 'Hi, I'm Bud Stone, and I wanted to say hello.' Bud had been looking for me at the request of mutual friends, and the split second glimpse of my name tag was all it took for him to take the risk which led to our enduring friendship.

"Thirty years later, the details of that meeting are still fresh. The event typifies the man—open, non-critical, confident—who could get other men to follow his lead in any endeavor. A laughing, completely honest demeanor, the ability to sort out the important from the 'small stuff',' and to instruct others in negotiating the pitfalls of four years on the 'rock.' Our friendship endured across regiments as Bud helped me in so many ways to get through and get educated and led me in principle and approach in the ensuing thirty years.

"I remember visits to his home, his gracious parents and an outstanding thirty-day leave in Europe. While we were on the Spanish island of Majorca two blond Swedish girls jumped on our rented Vespas, and we sped off to the nighttime beach with bottles of thirty-two cent 'champagne,' the culmination of every schoolboy's dream. Bud's fell in love—mine got cold and asked to be driven back home. In victory he was gracious, and gave me lessons in the 'ways of women,' rather than gloating, as was still politically correct in those halcyon days.

"I remember walking down the Cadet Chapel aisle, singing some goose-pimply battle hymn, past a resplendent Supe (superintendent of the academy) and staff, Bud's stentorian baritone leading the section. Then, disappearing into the woodwork, down the back stairs and out the side door and down the back stairwell to snatch forty minutes of freedom. While the Protestant Corps still sat prisoner to reverendly exhortation, we relaxed, read the paper or got ready to 'drag' (escort a young lady).

"I tried to talk Bud out of his dream of flying during that uncertain period. Being an Air Force Junior and safely selected for medical school, I knew that fanatic little men would try to kill my friend. In the heartsick days following the news of his heroic death, I faced a less final threat of demise. An enraged professor of surgery threatened to expel me because of a botched presentation of a patient case history. While waiting for the ultimate decision, I asked myself what Bud would have done. I marched into the man's 'den,' bearded the lion, and asked for another test of my fitness to serve. He consented, and I later finished the course with honors. I will always treasure the years of unqualified friendship that began with the words, 'Pssst. Hey, Rogers, follow me.' "

45

Dee Stone was truly a unique and exemplary individual. He was born in Forest Hills, New York, on 17 February 1943, the only son of Irene and Dee W. Stone, Sr., who already had two daughters, Mary and Grace. His father was a member of the New York City law firm, Chadbourne, Parks, Whiteside and Wolff and also a colonel in the Army Reserve. A World War I and World War II veteran, Dee, Sr., was serving in Africa with the Fourth Infantry Division when his son was born and later, on D day, landed on Utah Beach with the division's first wave. At an early age, son Dee proved to be a multitalented young lad, excelling in academics, athletics, and music. In addition to performing in school productions of Gilbert and Sullivan operettas, he was also invited to sing with the Boys' Choir of the Episcopal Church of the Heavenly Rest in New York City.

In 1955, with a desire to follow in his father's military footsteps, Dee entered the Manlius School where he continued his well-rounded development, participating in football, baseball, choir, double quartet, and Chapel Warden's Society. By the time he became a senior, he had risen to the position of brigade adjutant, and had garnered a number of awards including the Military Medal for distinguished achievement, the Degree of Champion and Commander of the Order of the Phoenix, the Rensselaer Polytechnic Institute Medal for Mathematics and the Bausch and Lomb Medal for Science.

During that senior year, Dee served as a shining example for several of his future West Point classmates. Chet Kempinski, who would later serve with Dee at Fort Carson, recalls that year: "I first met him at Manlius Prep School, an elite five-year boarding school, rather expensive, highly regarded, with a military environment. Manlius also happened to be one of the places where the Army Athletic Department sent approximately fifteen footballers (Nowak, Peterson, Beierschmitt, Kresefski, myself, etc.) each year for grooming in order to be competitive on a Division I basis. Anyway, Dee was the Brigade Adjutant, while we, as post grad students, were 'slick sleeves.' His military appearance was always immaculate and the rest of us learned a lot from Dee. We were proud to be his classmates during the ensuing four years. Those of us who were later assigned to the 1/19 Field Artillery with Dee got to know him and admire him even more. He would do anything for his friends and his country. His death proved that. It was a great loss for all of us." Dee graduated from Manlius in 1960 and joined the Class of 1964 that summer.

During his four years at West Point, he was vice president of the French Club, a member of the Astronomy Club, Math Forum, Rocket Society, Russian Club, and Chapel Choir. He also taught Sunday school for three years. And, possibly most important, Dee continued winning friendships and respect. Everyone loved him.

Upon graduation, Dee was commissioned into the artillery, as the branch was known at that time (in 1968 it would be split into two separate branches, air defense artillery and field artillery). One of the difficulties of the artillery, a highly technical branch, was the elimination of the basic course for Dee and his classmates, another experiment for the Class of '64. What had happened was that a few months before graduation it was announced to the class that for the USMA Classes of '64, '65, and '66, all graduates entering the army would attend Ranger School in lieu of their branch's basic course. The idea was that the mental and physical toughness acquired in Ranger School would be more beneficial than the technical knowledge learned in the basic course. It is not known if that belief proved to be true, but the policy was discontinued after the three-year test. As part of the deal, the army assured the class that its chain of command would be informed of the experiment so that commanders would understand some lack of technical knowledge and possibly provide that assistance for their new "Ranger" second lieutenants. When I reported to my artillery battalion commander in Germany, the lieutenant colonel had known nothing about such a program. After he told me what a stupid idea it was, he threw me out of his office.

It was not so bad for Dee while he and his classmates, Gary Johnson, Chet Kempinski, Paul Rennie, and Ron Williamson, served with the First Battalion, Nineteenth Field Artillery, of the Fifth Infantry Division in Fort Carson, Colorado. However, he had the itch to fly, so after about a year he attended flight training at Fort Wolters, Texas, and Fort Rucker, Alabama. That was against the best wishes of his classmates in the First of the Nineteenth, though, for they felt as Woody Rogers did, that Dee's daring and the danger of flying would be a risky combination. The four of them survived their tours in Vietnam and later became very successful in civilian life, most notably Ron Williamson, who after serving as the adjutant general (two stars) of South Dakota, rose to his current (at the time of this writing) position of president and CEO of Citibank.

Dee persisted, nevertheless, and after completing flight school in June 1966, was assigned to the 119th Aviation Company in Vietnam where he rapidly came to be recognized as an outstanding officer and a skillful helicopter pilot. Sadly, though, on 11 November 1966, one year and three days after his two former squad mates, Clair and David, died, Dee also made the supreme sacrifice while flying an escort mission in the Central Highlands. When called on to suppress enemy fire, he pulled out of formation, and, with no thought for his personal well-being, immediately directed the full firepower of his attack helicopter at the enemy heavy machine guns which were seriously endangering the troopships he was escorting. Dee accomplished his mission but it cost him his life. For his valor he was awarded the Distinguished Flying Cross and the Purple Heart to go along with the Air Medal with nine Oak Leaf Clusters, the National Order of the Republic of Vietnam and the Cross of Gallantry with Palm. He was later laid to rest at West Point with full military honors.

As was often the case during the Vietnam War, Dee's death caused significant confusion and grief within his family. One of his nephews, Paul Inwright, recently submitted the following: "To me my uncle was and always will be a hero—an example of one who fought the good fight in the wrong war. It must have been terrible for those who came back only to be scorned by Americans who should have been behind their fighting. It wasn't their fault the politicians of the era were idiots.

"My uncle was killed three days after my third birthday, so I really don't remember him, but I visit his grave twice a year, on Veterans Day and on his birthday. My uncle was my oldest brother's godfather. John was eleven when Bud was killed; he was watching a professional hockey game when my father told him that Bud wasn't coming home. Since then John has not been able to watch a hockey game, and he is a sports nut. As for me, I will always mourn the loss of the very special uncle I never got to know.

"As for my grandfather, who chased Pancho Villa with 'Black Jack' Pershing, landed on D day to save civilization as we know it from what would surely have been insanity, and came through all of this unscathed, the death of his only son put him almost immediately into traumatic senility in which he spent the last fourteen years of his life.

"Because of Bud's death I also lost my grandfather. The most unfortunate thing for me, for my brothers, for my mother, for her sister, for my grandmother and grandfather, for all those who knew him, and for the United States Army is that we all will never know the great accomplishments that would have been."

Many other families would be similarly affected during the next several years as our losses continued to mount. The fact that the enemy's losses were many times greater has not been any consolation. Eighteen more of Dee's classmates would perish in Vietnam within the following five years. They were all painful.

49

For those of us who knew him, his final action was Dee at his best, wanting to take the chance, knowing the danger, but also knowing that his actions might allow others to live. We knew him as a slightly overweight plebe who would take seemingly suicidal chances to help another classmate; as a trimmed-down yearling who became a serious, yet ever-exuberant young man; as a cow who became a resourceful and imaginative companion; and as a firstie, a well-rounded, handsome, energetic contemporary who could, in a few seconds, give more reasons for life than many had given in a lifetime.

To his parents, Dee was the only son, who grew up quickly and who was the pleasure of their lives. To his sisters, Dee was the little brother who was their pride and joy in life and a monument to them in death. To his nephews and nieces, he was a hero whom they wish they could have known for much longer. To his friends, Dee represented friendship at its finest. He lived life to the fullest and symbolized the wonders, happiness, and freedom for which America stands.

Chapter Seven

James Conrad Powers

This big Iowa farm boy came to us by way of the Merchant Marine Academy, where he spent one year. His large smile and amiable personality are matched only by his drive and ability as a leader. His sincerity and good nature are attested to by the number of true friends that Jim has made while here at the Academy.

At the beginning of 1967, the U.S. troop strength in Vietnam was approximately 380,000. By the end of the year it had grown to 500,000. The Class of 1964's combat losses increased by a slightly higher ratio during that year. Five members of the class would perish in 1967 compared to the three who died in 1966. In a way, that is surprising, because on 3 January 1967, after thirteen months as first lieutenants, almost everyone in the class in the army was promoted to the rank of captain. The promotion date would have been 3 June (eighteen months as a second lieutenant and eighteen months as a first lieutenant), but with the war's escalation promotions were speeded up. Eventually, the time in grade requirement would reach twelve months for each lieutenant rank, resulting in officers becoming captains in exactly two years. Theoretically, captains should have a lower casualty rate than lieutenants since lieutenants, as platoon leaders, are closer to the front lines. However, with the general absence of front lines in Vietnam, that theory did not always apply.

On 26 May 1967 James C. Powers became the seventh warrior of the Class of '64 to die in combat, and the first captain to die. He was also the first victim who was married, leaving his wife, Ann, a widow. Their daughter, Jamie, would be born less than four months later on 15 September.

Jim was born in Dubuque, Iowa, on 23 April 1940, the second of eight children—six boys and two girls. (The Powers family and the Graham (Chapter 24) family were the largest of all among '64's fallen warriors.) His mother, Martha, was of German heritage and his father, Philip, was of Irish ancestry. Jim inherited all the best qualities from both parents.

52

Jim was a true Iowa farm boy. He grew up on the family's 150-acre farm just outside the city limits. It was a huge endeavor which, besides several crops and a large dairy herd, included beef cattle, hogs, chickens, goats, banty hens, and later, during Jim's high school years, sheep. According to family lore, it was the sheep which caused Jim to finalize his decision to become a soldier.

On the farm, Jim learned every aspect of farming and always entered at least one animal in competition at the annual fair. When he was in the seventh grade, his father was hospitalized in the Mayo Clinic for almost five months. During this time Jim and his brothers Dave and Paul took over the operation of the farm. It was a challenging situation for the three youngsters, but they managed to keep the family fed and the livestock alive without any regression in their schoolwork.

Jim attended St. Anthony's Grade School where he was under the tutelage of the Sisters of the Blessed Virgin Mary. The school was only a mile and a half from the farm and Jim's parents always brought fresh vegetables and meats to the good Sisters. Although they were altar boys, Jim and his brothers were frequently corrected for causing disturbances or teasing girls. However, their mother always assured the nuns that it was just good-natured fun and that her sons were as innocent as they looked. In fact, they did have very angelic appearances.

The Powers boys were constantly on the move. After mastering trikes, wagons, bikes, and horses, they began experimenting with their father's Case Tractor and subjected it to every test known to man, agricultural and otherwise. While in high school Jim's younger brother Dave developed a love of cars and racing. When the farm chores were completed, Jim and Dave would work on their cars—usually with the help of a cute city girl standing by to pass tools to them. Jim and his brothers worked hard and played hard. There was never a dull moment.

Jim attended Loras Academy High School and worked each summer for farmers in the area. His main extracurricular activities during that time included being president of the 4-H club and a junior ROTC cadet. Jim would later say that his interest in a military career began while he was in the ROTC program, mainly because of the influence of an outstanding infantry officer instructor, Captain Leo O'Brien.

By the time he graduated in 1958, he made up his mind to go to West Point, but the college board examinations indicated that he needed a little more preparation in math and science. So, Jim enrolled in Northwestern Prep School in Minneapolis. Because he could not afford the tuition, he was given a free room in the attic and did kitchen and housekeeping work in order to pay his bills. After that year he attended the Merchant Marine Academy in Kings Point, New York, thus moving closer to his goal, mentally and physically. With his academic and leadership credentials significantly strengthened, Jim was awarded an appointment to the United States Military Academy by Congressman James Bromwell in 1960.

The new cadet's departure from the train station was a grand ordeal, especially since he was the only one in the family who had ever been east of Chicago. It would turn out to be a bittersweet farewell for the large entourage that sent Jim off to his military dream.

Jim's four years at West Point were notable for the number of friends he made. From the day he arrived in New Cadet Barracks with his long farmer's stride and wide smile to his firstie year as a cadet captain and K-2 company commander, no one was more liked. His two years in K-2 were shared with another class standout, Alex Hottell (Chapter 22), who would also perish in Vietnam, three years after Jim.

As a plebe and yearling, Jim belonged to Company I-2. In fact, I-2 had a Jim Powers, '64, for all four years. When James C. Powers went to K-2 with the 1962 company shuffle, James W. Powers was assigned to I-2. For many in the class, when the name Jim Powers was mentioned, the question would follow, "Which one?" The answer would usually be, "The blond one (James C.)" or "The dark-haired one (James W.)." It would become a very poignant point when Jim was killed.

Jim was an extremely active cadet. Besides playing B Squad lacrosse, he was a member of the Honor Committee, the Hop Committee, Russian Club, Catholic Chapel Acolytes, Catholic Choir, Cardinal Newman Forum, and the Outdoor Sportsman Club. He also loved a good time in New York City and the German-American Club on Third Avenue in Manhattan was never too far away. When Jim returned from his summer assignment in Germany between yearling and cow years, he and several classmates wore their recently purchased lederhosen to an Irish bar in The Rockaways, pretending they were German students studying in the United States. Jim felt that was a surefire way to meet girls.

He did meet numerous young ladies as a cadet, but none were right for him. Jim was responsible, however, for at least two marriages in the class. One of his former roommates, Kevin Kelley, relates the following: "One Sunday morning during the spring of 1962 I was sitting with my date in the Weapons Room (a cadet club) when Jim walked in, escorting a cute young lady named Rosemary. He introduced us and explained that he was just going to sit with her until her date returned from the first regiment chapel formation in about an hour. That was sufficient time for me to convince Rosemary to go out with me the following weekend and we got married a few years later.

"Jim also introduced his sister Jeanne to our classmate Brendan Quann after the Army-Air Force football game in the fall of 1963. Their wedding took place on 28 October 1967, five months after Jim's death."

While Jim was a cadet, he and his family looked forward to his summer leaves. He loved his family and relished each moment with them and they with him. However, his mother never understood how someone could be so neat at school and yet so sloppy at home. So, as a treat for her, Jim would manicure the yard as if it were the superintendent's quarters. Although he mowed the lawn with the farm tractor, he sharpened his leadership skills by having his younger sister and brothers do the weeding, trimming, and sweeping. One summer while Jim was helping his dad on the farm, he was struck on the head by a large oak tree they were uprooting. He returned to West Point not only with the painful memory, but also a very large scar across his head.

Following graduation Jim was commissioned in the infantry. His maturity and work experience benefitted him greatly in his successful completion of the Airborne and Ranger courses. In all probability, those schools never saw a more good-natured candidate with a better disposition. He was a joy to be with, even under the most trying circumstances.

Jim's first assignment took him to Fort Lewis, Washington, where he met, fell in love with, and married Ann Wilson of Mount Vernon, Washington. Ann was a senior at the University of Washington when they met, and Jim's '64 Chevy put on many miles between Fort Lewis and Seattle until they were wed on 18 December 1965 in Ann's hometown. They packed more living into the first six months of their marriage than most people do in a lifetime. Jim knew he would be deploying soon with the Fourth Infantry Division as it was about to join the build-up of U.S. Forces in Vietnam.

As expected, the orders came a few months after the wedding, and in June 1966 Jim left for Southeast Asia. He served as a general's aide for the first six months, all the time hoping that he would have the chance to command a company since he would be getting promoted to captain in early January. After meeting Ann in Hawaii for R&R (rest and recuperation) in December, Jim's wish came true and he took command of Company C, Third Battalion, Eighth Infantry Regiment. It was hazardous duty, to say the least, but Jim was prepared for the challenge. Sadly, though, on 26 May 1967, only about a month shy of his scheduled departure, Jim met his fate he-

56

roically near the top of Hill 571, west of Pleiku. He had been leading his company up the hill to link up with B Company at the summit. Only eighty yards from the top, Jim called for a rest break so his troops could recover their strength before the final upward surge. Within minutes, however, all hell broke loose. C Company had stumbled into a North Vietnamese Army battalion which had prepared an ambush for the approaching Americans. Automatic weapons fire and mortar rounds began to saturate the area. Jim was killed immediately as the first wave of Communist assault troops moved forward. In fact, all the officers of the company were either killed or wounded so the first sergeant, Richard Childers, had to take control and lead the counterattack. It took over three hours at a cost of nine killed and forty-eight wounded, but the topkick bravely and skillfully accomplished the mission.

Several U.S. newspapers published accounts of the encounter, citing Jim's outstanding application of training and tactics which insured his men against quick annihilation. During the march before the ambush, he had repeatedly ordered the men of his platoons to keep a good tactical formation, even though their proximity to B Company and the summit of Hill 571 seemed to preclude the probability of an enemy attack. Consequently, the lead men maintained a true course, slashing their way through the jungle with powerful swings of their machetes, while the remainder of the company maintained the proper tactical spacing.

The North Vietnamese commander probably had not counted on such discipline, as U.S. troops often tended to get sloppy as they neared real or imagined safety. But Jim had not let that happen to Charlie Company. Had the company been strung out in a line or overly bunched up, the Communist commander might well have been the first to destroy a major American unit.

Despite losing his own life, Jim's forethought and firm leadership saved his command. He was awarded the Silver Star, the Purple Heart, and the Soldier's Medal for his gallantry, as well as several Vietnamese awards. He is buried at Evergreen Washelli Memorial Cemetery in Seattle, Washington. Jim was the only '64 warrior to die while serving with the Fourth Infantry Division.

Five months later, when Jim's sister Jeanne and Brendan Quann were married, Ann Powers was a member of the wedding party. In spite of her grief, she told herself life had to continue. Also in that wedding party was another classmate, Bill Reynolds, supposedly a confirmed bachelor. As fate would have it, Ann's and Bill's paths later crossed and in time they fell in love and got married, eventually giving Jamie a sister, two brothers, and a loving family. Jamie is now married to Michael Rector and they have a son of their own, Jim's grandchild, Hunter.

The Captain James C. Powers Scholarship Fund was established by Ann and the Powers family following his death. It has awarded scholarships to deserving graduates of St. Anthony's Grade School every year since Jim's death.

Although Jim's mother and father have since joined him, he is still survived by his sisters: Kathryn Miller of Champaign, Illinois, and Jeanne Quann of Dubuque; and five brothers: Dave of Houston, Texas; Paul of Denver, Colorado; Pat of Dubuque; Tom of Seattle, Washington; and John (Jay), also of Denver.

The extended Powers clan has frequent reunions and remembering Jim is always a central theme. Jim's many friends in the Class of '64 and the U.S. Army also remember him as a compassionate leader and a great friend. He unselfishly gave his life so others could be free.

Chapter Eight

James Clifford McKittrick

Quietly efficient and capable, Cliff has made a deep and last-
ing impression on all those who had the pleasure of knowing
him. The "Southern Gentleman From Clennon" has excelled
in all that he has attempted while at West Point. This habit
will, undoubtedly, follow him through his future years.

Sometime after the Vietnam Cease-fire Agreement of 27 January 1973, the government of North Vietnam released the names of the American prisoners it held and began making preparations for their return. For those families who had loved ones on the list, it was a time of ecstasy. However, it was a tremendous letdown for some other families—those whose loved ones were missing in action but whose names did not appear on the list. One such family was that of Army Captain Cliff McKittrick, who had been missing since 18 June 1967. Cliff's brother Jack, of Camden, South Carolina, said, "As the months and years went on, we realized that it was more and more doubtful that he could be alive, but still we had hope that he was a prisoner. That was the best we could hope for. As the war came to a close, the names of prisoners were released and he was not one of them coming home. That was a pretty rough time." Then, in early 1975, the family received a telegram and letter from the Department of the Army stating that, "Army records are being amended to change your son's status from missing to that of deceased as of 22 January 1975. ... This date is not an actual or probable date of death, but it is a date established in accordance with the law." The army also posthumously promoted Cliff to major.

On the day Cliff disappeared, the battery he commanded had been shelling an enemy position in the Chu Lai area of South Vietnam. He and his first sergeant boarded an OH-23 helicopter at 5:25 P.M. for the purpose of conducting a visual reconnaissance to assess the damage his battery had inflicted, a mission that was scheduled to terminate by 6:10. After taking off, the helicopter was never heard from. Searches were begun that night and continued by air and ground for four days. Loudspeaker aircraft were utilized and leaflets were disseminated offering a reward for information concerning the helicopter. Unconfirmed information was received that a helicopter had gone down due to mechanical failure and that the three persons on board had been killed by the Viet Cong and the helicopter dismantled and hidden in the river. However, a thorough search of the area revealed no evidence to substantiate this report. Cliff's good boyhood friend, R. E. (Sonny) Elmore, Jr., flew over that area about a year later and stated that, "It is very difficult terrain— It has the capacity to swallow up small aircraft." At the time of his disappearance, Cliff was four days short of his twenty-fifth birthday. He had only been in Vietnam for three weeks.

Cliff and his two brothers, Dan (six years older) and Jack (four years younger), grew up on a family-size dairy farm between Laurens and Clinton, South Carolina. Their father, Kenneth, was a farmer/builder and a lifetime Baptist deacon. Their mother, Inez, worked around the clock, both helping with the farm and running the house. Cousin Betty Smith remembers those times: "Some of my happiest moments are of us children playing in a creek that was close to Cliff's house. It may seem so simple now, but it was fun to spend the afternoon playing in Duncan Creek. Crackers, peanut butter, and Kool-Aid were a real treat and will never taste the same as they did then. Cliff and his brother Jack coaxed me to cross a 'footlog' across this creek, and I felt like I had really done something special.

"Cliff was a down-to-earth person. Even though he achieved many high honors, he never lost sight of the important things in life. He truly cared about his family and friends and his church. He had a quiet way about him, but he had a great influence on people in a positive way.

"His determination was unique. He set goals for himself in academics, athletics and personal goals and always achieved them.

61

"A perfect example of his compassion for others was when his mother passed away. We all loved her dearly, and we were so grieved. Cliff made a special effort to comfort us, even though he was hurting so himself."

Another cousin, Evelyn Batson, recalls their youth together: "...riding Bonnie, the family horse, or loading the pickup truck for a two-mile trip to Yarbers Mill. There, in a bend of the river, was a tall tree with a rope for swinging over the river. Many hours were spent in this swimming hole. One memory of our childhood was the McKittrick family goat. Nothing gave Dan and Cliff more pleasure than turning that goat loose on their female cousins. There was no way to get away from that goat. I remember climbing on top of an automobile and the goat came right up behind me. I ran in the house, but what do Dan and Cliff do but let that goat in the house. He chased us all the way up the stairs, those long horns right behind us.

"Cliff was brought up in a Christian home, to work hard, and to love, respect and rely on his Christian values in life. ... I sum up Cliff's life by saying that he lived every day of his life to the fullest. He was truly a man of compassion and great character. Cliff was the pride of his friends and family. Needless to say, it was hard when we received the message, 'Missing in Action.' "

Cliff's schooling began at Oak Grove, a rural two-room school that housed seven grades. His classmate there, Dr. William Harris, presently the pastor of the First Baptist Church in Greenwood, said, "The thing I remember most about him was his honesty and industry." Sonny Elmore noted that, "He was never much interested in farming because he was much more at home with an idea." Cliff was the type who did not like to squander anything, especially time, so he kept himself extremely busy. Besides schoolwork, sports and the farm chores, he also sold the *True Grit* newspaper. It was well known that, although he was studious, Cliff was not a constant bookworm and was very popular among his classmates.

In fact, he graduated as the class salutatorian from Clinton High School in 1960, having made only one B to besmirch his record of straight A's. He was also a star athlete and the president of his class. Another classmate, Mrs. Charlton Law of Columbia (the former Linda Milam of Clinton) said, "I get chills standing here thinking of him because his death was so untimely. He was such a well-regarded person." Cliff's record at Clinton High was so outstanding that his brother Jack, upon beginning classes there three months after Cliff graduated, went by the principal's office and said, "I want to tell you one thing. Don't expect Cliff's grades out of me."

Cliff continued to excel in all areas at West Point as a member of the Class of 1964. Besides being known as a true "Southern Gentleman," he was highly respected as a well-rounded performer and a natural leader. Among his many extracurricular activities was the Honor Committee, probably the most important cadet organization of all. As a first classman, Cliff served as the executive officer of the first regiment, one of only nine five-stripers in the class.

After graduating in the top twenty-five percent of the class, Cliff attended the Airborne and Ranger courses and then reported to the First Battalion, 320th Field Artillery of the Eighty-second Airborne Division at Fort Bragg. Jeff Kleb, USMA '64, was also assigned to the 1/320th and recalls their time together there: "I hadn't known Cliff well as a cadet since we were in different regiments, but after spending our first year in the army together in the Eighty-second Airborne Division it became clear that he was an extraordinary individual—level headed, loved by all, patriotic, tough, and determined. We both started out in the battalion with a problem, however—we knew nothing about artillery since we hadn't been to the basic course. Luckily, though, a great NCO, then Sergeant First Class Carroll Crain, took us aside and offered to tutor us (he also didn't want us to be a detriment to the battalion). So, for the next several months, after duty hours, he pounded all the aspects of field artillery gunnery into our heads. It was a tremendous effort on his part, and Cliff and I worked like dogs to make up for what we'd missed, which we eventually did. Carroll Crain was a real professional who later rose to be the command sergeant major of the Eighty-second Airborne Division Artillery.

"Socially, Cliff was the penultimate bachelor whose bachelor pad was a relaxing place for lots of us junior officers to get together. Conversely, he was so likeable that all the wives loved having him come home with their husbands for dinner. He was the perfect guest and quite well fed.

"Cliff and I spent our last six months together in the Eighty-second in the Dominican Republic where we did a lot of artillery training and parachuting. Charlie Hutchison's death there was a shock to both of us. Later, when I was in Vietnam and heard that Cliff was missing it tore me up. I hoped that he'd been captured because I knew that if anyone could escape, he could. I won't stop hoping for a miracle until there is positive identification of his remains. All of us in the class feel that way. Cliff was the cream of the crop and a true friend."

In the spring of 1967 Cliff deployed to Vietnam and took command of a firing battery in the Third Battalion, Sixteenth Field Artillery. The 3/16th was part of Task Force Oregon, which would be activated as the American Division on 25 September of that year. Cliff was just beginning to get comfortable as a battery commander when he, his first sergeant, and the helicopter pilot disappeared.

Another report that reached the McKittrick family in the months that followed was one that said the helicopter had been shot down, dismantled, and buried in a riverbank, and that Cliff had been taken prisoner. His older brother, Dan, expressed the family's hope: "He was a paratrooper and a ranger, and we knew that if anybody could survive, he could. But after a month or so, it began to sink in that he might not be coming back. But we still had hope. We still do. There's a little spot there."

More than 2,000 Americans remain missing from the war in Southeast Asia. Even though in most of the cases there is no indication that the missing person survived, their families have to maintain a "spot of hope." In Cliff's case, the area where he disappeared is now under water. However, until his remains are identified, there will still be some hope in a lot of hearts.

Despite their loss in Vietnam, both Dan and Jack McKittrick have said they stand behind their country's military efforts in that war and others. Jack summarized: "I thought like a lot of other Americans, that it was the right thing to do to keep Communism in check. ... I think we all learned that...if we send our soldiers out to fight, we should let them win it and use whatever they need to defeat the enemy and get home."

Cliff McKittrick was the epitome of a professional soldier and was destined for great things in the army. He was an inspiration to all those who knew him and a totally dedicated officer and gentleman.

Betty Smith continues: "It was always a tradition for us to have a family Christmas dinner every year and one of our uncles always returned thanks. I don't know why, but on Christmas Day of 1966, someone asked Cliff to return thanks, and he did. His prayer was very special and sincere. That was the last Christmas Cliff was with us.

"I remember the day we got word that Cliff was missing in action. This just couldn't happen to Cliff! What a sad time for all the family, so much grief, so much heartache.

"I feel privileged to have had Cliff for my cousin. I still think about him with the fondest memories. He was and still is loved."

[For the chronological purposes of this book, Cliff's MIA date of 18 June 1967, when his loss began to be felt, is being considered rather than his death declaration date, which was nearly eight years later.]

Chapter Nine

David Allan Bujalski

Our military monastery captured Buj from St. John's (Minnesota) after two years. Spartan life fitted him perfectly? Ole Buj has proved "in there" for coaching H-2's academic and social goats. His mental and physical acumen and very pro fiancee, will take him far.

S ir, New Cadet Bujalski reports to Mister Dreesbach, the first sergeant of the First New Cadet Company, for the first time as ordered."

"Very good, mister," replied the cadet first sergeant, as he checked the name off his list. "Now squeeze that neck in and report back to your squad leader!"

New Cadet David Allan Bujalski felt momentarily proud that he was able to report in correctly on his first attempt, word for word. After all, while he had been standing in line to do so, he observed that almost all of his classmates ahead of him had stumbled over the words and had been sent to the end of the line to try again. As he hustled back to rejoin his squad, he realized that was only one obstacle of many he would have to overcome that day, the first day of "Beast Barracks" at the United States Military Academy. He still had to get a haircut (a "Beast" skinning), learn how to march, get fitted for his uniforms, shine his shoes, polish brass, put away a ton of clothing and other items that had been dumped on his bed, and then march in formation to Trophy Point for the swearing in ceremony.

It was an incredibly hectic day, but, almost miraculously, the six new cadet companies of the Class of 1964, clad in gray wool (the lighter weight cotton uniforms came out years later), appeared in formation and were marched by the upperclass cadre to Trophy Point where they swore allegiance to their country. As David was marching back to South Area, his stomach reminded him that supper time was approaching. At six feet three and over two hundred pounds, this young man was accustomed to hearty meals, and the few tiny bites of lunch he was permitted did little to fill the void inside. Supper was no better, however, as David and his classmates found them-

67

selves passing food and drinks, being screamed at, and eating very little. Some new cadets, who had no previous military connections, were practically in a state of shock at the treatment they were receiving. Even though David had an older brother who graduated from West Point (Jack, Class of '58) and told him what to expect, the firsthand experience was a definite jolt. As David hungrily marched back to his room, he wondered what would happen that evening. He was hoping there would be time for him and his two roommates to organize the mess in their room and start putting a good military "spit" shine on their boots and shoes. He knew there probably wouldn't be time for a movie as one of his unaware classmates had suggested before checking in that morning.

Upon arriving back in the room, David heard his squad leader's voice bellowing, "All you dumb smacks report to my room immediately!" As they stood, bracing, a few minutes later, the squad leader informed them that they were dirty and smelly, but the training schedule had a solution for such a problem. Each evening at a designated time a shower formation would be held and the first one would begin in five minutes. The shower formation would be conducted as follows: each new cadet would stand at a rigid position of attention in front of his locker in the sinks (basement). The uniform would be slippers and bathrobe, with the left hand extended, holding a soapbox and having a towel neatly folded over the wrist. When a new cadet's bathrobe was quite soaked with sweat, he would be given permission to take a short shower. At first David thought it might take all night to get sweaty enough for a shower, but he soon found out that this was something in which he excelled. As the upperclassmen jumped around, screaming at the plebes, David kept squeezing his neck in and tensing his big body. Once the beads of sweat started popping out, they didn't stop. Invariably, during that summer, David was one of the first to take a shower and get back to his room. This gave him extra time to take care of other duties that those who didn't sweat well often never got to.

After "Beast Barracks" David was assigned to Company M-2, where, as a flanker, he fit in just fine. As a group, the plebes in the Mighty Deuce felt quite fortunate to be there. Life as a plebe was not easy anywhere, but it was well known to be more bearable in M-2 than in most other companies. Perhaps David and his plebe-company mates were a little too comfortable, however. One time during the winter, when they were marching in formation past the mess hall to the library, the classmate in charge of the group said, "Let's do a Buckner Rocket!" The Rocket is a cadet cheer which goes, "(Whistle) - BOOM! - Ahhh, USMA Rah! Rah! USMA Rah! Rah! Hoo - Rah! Hoo - Rah! AR - MAY! Rah! Team! Team! Team!" The Buckner Rocket, starting with the same whistle, goes, "BOOM! - Ahhh, SHIT!"

When the twenty-eight or so M-2 plebes rendered their extremely loud Buckner Rocket, the formation was immediately halted by a nearby officer. By the time they returned to the barracks, the company tactical officer and an irate group of cadet leaders were waiting to tear into the bold young plebes. They were promised an appropriate punishment which turned out to be a hike through the academy hills the following Sunday afternoon, in combat gear. Such a hike would have been difficult enough on a cold day, but it just happened to have snowed about two feet that weekend. It was a rough trek, especially for the not-so-tall Southerners. But for long-legged David from North Dakota, it was a walk in the park. The worst part of the entire ordeal, though, was that they had to spend practically the whole evening cleaning their rifles, equipment, and boots.

During his four years as a cadet, David earned the respect and admiration of his classmates through his unselfish giving of time and effort in academic coaching, his active participation in extracurricular activities and intramural sports, and his own academic achievements. He was always on the Dean's List and graduated in the top third of the class.

David was from a strong family who considered service to God and country above all else. He was born on 18 August 1940 in Valley City, North Dakota, the youngest of six children born to Gladys and John Bujalski. At first he was called "Little David" but it wasn't long before that nickname disappeared, as he outgrew his older siblings. The development of his character kept pace with his physical growth and he became a cheerful, friendly, loveable young giant.

David's faith in God manifested itself in his early teens. He spent his last three years of high school at St. John's High in Collegeville, Minnesota, preparing for the priesthood. However, during his senior year he realized he did not have a religious vocation. He continued at St. John's University for two more years, majoring in physics and trying to decide how he could best serve his fellow man. During that time one of David's brothers was at West Point and another was at the Air Force Academy. David was deeply impressed with the influence those institutions had on his brothers and with the work his brothers were doing, so, he decided to follow in their footsteps.

Upon graduation, David was commissioned in the artillery. Three days later he married Barbara DePretoro, whom he had met during yearling year while she was a student at Ladycliff College, just outside the gate in Highland Falls (it has since closed down, the property was bought by the government and is presently utilized by various USMA agencies). The honeymoon came to an abrupt halt when David had to depart for Ranger School in early August. He didn't have any major problems there, but his Ranger buddy, Howie Bachman, who was about forty-five pounds lighter than David, had some difficult moments during hand-to-hand combat training and rappelling down the cliff with David on his back.

70

After Airborne School, the young couple was off to Munich, Germany, for David's first and only artillery assignment. While there, daughter Elizabeth Marie was born in July of 1965. In June 1966 they moved to Fort Huachuca, Arizona, where David became the commander of C Company, First Combat Support Training Brigade. A year later he transferred to the Corps of Engineers and shortly thereafter left for Vietnam to join the Sixty-fifth Engineer Battalion of the Twenty-fifth Infantry Division. As was typical of the men of '64, David felt it was his duty to go there—since we were there, we had a job to do. On 15 August 1967, only eight days after his arrival, David fell victim to a sniper's bullet while performing a helicopter-borne road-reconnaissance mission. It was less than two months after another aircraft tragedy—the disappearance of Cliff McKittrick. Six weeks later, daughter Kathleen Ann was born in Glen Cove, Long Island, New York.

David was posthumously awarded the Bronze Star and Purple Heart medals, and on 27 March 1968 "Bujalski Field" was dedicated in his honor at Fort Huachuca. A stone monument, with a memorial plaque on top, was constructed there by the men in his company. On 29 October 1971 a rededication ceremony was held at a newly completed lighted football field with an all-weather track near the field house.

Throughout his military career, as a cadet and as an officer, David developed at a tremendous rate. The friendly young giant from North Dakota became a dedicated, skillful, highly qualified officer. In the words of his first sergeant at Fort Huachuca, "He was revered by his cadre, loved by his students, and respected by his superiors."

I was one of David's many good friends and I always felt it was a joy and a privilege to be in M-2 with Dave during plebe and yearling years. He was a star among us, truly a gentle giant who was highly respected by all, upperclassmen, underclassmen, and classmates alike. Big and strong, smart, level-headed, decent, selfless—that was Dave. Everyone admired him.

71

We were on the intramural water polo team together during yearling year. Our team was great—we only lost one of eleven games—to the eventual brigade champions. Basically, though, we were a one-man team—David Bujalski. He probably made ninety percent of our goals. I can still picture him, rising up out of the water like a big whale and firing a bullet into the net. Goaltenders were terrified of him.

I remember the last time I saw him. It was the spring of 1966. I was sitting in my office in Gelnhausen, Germany, and in walked Dave, wearing his field gear. His unit was conducting a field training exercise in the vicinity, so he dropped by for a cup of coffee. We talked about old times, current times, and the future. We lamented the combat losses of Hutch, Clair, and David and acknowledged that we would soon see combat also. That Dave would die in Vietnam, though, was the furthest thing from my mind.

A few years later, my wife and I were driving through Arizona and we took a side trip to Fort Huachuca to see Bujalski Field. It is a fitting tribute to a most deserving American who gave it all for his country just as he gave it all for his family and friends for almost twenty-seven years.

David's life was too short for him to have reached his full potential. We can only conjecture as to what he would have achieved, but we do know that he influenced the lives of those who knew him. David was a man for all seasons and was big not only in size, but mentally, morally, and spiritually as well. The strength which his outer form so forcefully displayed was only a picture of his inner strength of character. An army chaplain and close friend of David's wrote the following words, which epitomize the regard we all had for David, "One of God's Saints has come and gone and richer is the world which he passed through."

David does live on, though, in his daughters and in his grandson, David Anthony Chiariello, who was born on 26 July 1994, the son of Elizabeth and her husband, Dominic. Barbara, who has had the good fortune to marry Jack Drinane,

brought her family, including young David, to the Class of
'64's thirtieth reunion in October 1994 at West Point. He was
a robust three-month-old and one look at him left no doubt
about who his maternal grandfather was. If he grows up to
be anything like his grandfather, he'll be a great man.

Chapter Ten

Michael James Kiley

Airborne, ranger, and bachelor are all Mike's goals in life. Woe be to the girl that catches Mike. She will have to be a hunter, a handball and a tennis player. Never in the rack when there was an open handball court, Mike was an avid handball fan. Other free time was spent shooting at and missing grouse.

If anyone ever epitomized being a warrior, it was Mike Kiley. To those who knew him well, he at first seemed to be a cheerful and friendly, yet somewhat reserved, Californian, and indeed, he was that. However, when the going got tough, Mike's own toughness took over and would always serve as a model for all. This was evident in his youth, during his cadet days, in Ranger School, and during his short but illustrious army career.

Mike embodied the ideals of decency, integrity, and professionalism. As a human being, he was an example for mankind. As a soldier, he possessed the "sacred fire" Napoleon believed so important in his officers.

Mike's tactical officer at West Point referred to him as "a young Patton"; his company commander during his first Vietnam tour called him "the bravest man in action he had ever seen"; his first platoon sergeant, who worked for him in Korea, said Mike was "the best officer he had ever worked for"; his platoon sergeant in Vietnam (first tour) cited him as "an unusually skilled infantry officer to whom he always looked for advice, especially when dealing with the lower enlisted." Mike's brother Kevin says he was "undoubtedly the most honest person I ever met. He believed in telling the truth, no matter what the consequences. ... He was the ideal big brother-teacher, friend, and mentor." Growing up, Kevin had several learning experiences with Mike about doing what's right.

West Point classmate Richard Carr also had such an encounter, as he recalls:

"About midway through our first-class year, I had my wisdom teeth removed. As part of the healing process, I was called back to the hospital for a check by the surgeon. The appointment ended midway through my first period military

75

history class, and I thought, 'Why not go back to my room and sleep? I was authorized to be at the dentist—surely no one is going to question me beyond the appointment.

"Somewhat later in the day came a knock at the door of my room. It was Mike Kiley. He was section leader of my military history class. 'Were you authorized to be absent from the history class?' My response: 'I had an appointment with the dental surgeon concerning my recently extracted wisdom teeth.' (I'm off the hook, right? Wrong!) 'Did the appointment last the whole period?' Why did anyone have to be so fastidious with their duties?

"I subsequently spent considerable time on the area contemplating the concept of duty. Mike Kiley had a complete dedication to 'what was right.' Mike had already had the opportunity to walk the area—for a total of five hours. Out of curiosity, he and a buddy once got into some trouble on purpose to see what it was like. They did not enjoy it and regretted the experience."

From an early age, Mike showed exemplary dedication and responsibility. His mother, Eileen, recounts the following episodes:

"Michael was about three and a half when he and I took a train to Seattle to meet his dad (Francis Marion Kiley, Captain, U.S. Naval Reserve, served in both World Wars and was returning home after being the captain of the USS *Spica* in the Pacific during World War II). His ship docked there and little Michael decided he would be a sailor after he boarded and met all the sailors. When we arrived home he insisted on a sailor outfit, so he and his younger brother (John Patrick, a marine colonel at the time of this writing, served as a rifle company commander in Vietnam in 1968-1969 and also served on the First Marine Expeditionary Force staff during Operation Desert Storm, the liberation of Kuwait.) became sailors. ... They had the complete outfit—cap, shoes, etc., and wore them everywhere. Later, they became soldiers, and even carried wooden rifles.

76

"Michael was in kindergarten and the war was over, so he became a cowboy. His dad made sure he and his brother had the full regalia, hat, boots, leather chaps, ropes, etc., and he would take them, dressed so, with a playmate to a cowboy movie every Saturday.

"He was in first grade when he came home one day and told me I had to visit his teacher. He was in trouble. On Monday I met his teacher and she had forgotten what it was all about. Then she said, 'Oh, I had to pretend I would punish him but I was so glad he hit the other boy in the nose. He really deserved it.'

"Once when the paperboy came to collect his money Michael decided he wanted to be a paperboy. When we moved to Long Beach he was offered a job delivering papers. We thought he was too young, but his dad said, 'If you take the job you have to stay with it,' and he did for several years. It was good training and he never shirked anything he undertook.

"Kevin (Kevin Francis, USMA '76, a major in the U.S. Marine Corps Reserve at the time of this writing, served as fire direction officer in the Tenth Marine Regiment during the Persian Gulf Conflict. His was one of the first units into occupied Kuwait, arriving the day before the allied invasion.) was born when Michael was eleven years old and Patrick ten. The two of them and Anne Litschi, who was Michael's age, were the godparents. Michael took this very seriously. He always looked after Kevin, and as Kevin grew older, he would advise him. Theirs was a good relationship. On Fathers' Day when Michael was in Korea, after their father had died, Kevin asked me if it would be all right to send Mike a Fathers' Day card. When Michael's things were returned to me the card was there with his other mementoes. I imagine they were the youngest godparents ever.

"When Michael was sixteen his father, who was port captain for Mobil Oil on the West Coast, put him aboard one of the tankers that sailed from Long Beach to Seattle. He learned

77

to love the sea and told me that after the army he thought he would work for his captain's license. He would go to sea every summer and once even during Christmas vacation.

"Michael was a great dancer and played the piano. After graduating from St. Anthony's High School in Long Beach he attended Loyola University in Los Angeles for a year. He told me later that it was the best year of his life. We all enjoyed having him home on weekends and every Wednesday he would visit his grandmother. It was the highlight of her week and they had always been close to each other. Her son, my brother, had died aboard the Pan American Clipper that exploded in the South Seas and he filled that void for her. Mike was very like my brother in a number of ways."

Kevin remembers the following incident during Mike's year at Loyola:

"He was joining a fraternity and among the rites of initiation the freshmen had to go down to Main Street in Los Angeles and 'procure' a G-string from one of the establishments that featured strippers. He was not too thrilled to go down there (nor was our mother about him going)—then, as now, it was quite unsavory—so, our mom took out her sewing basket and made him one out of lace and powdered it to look somewhat worn. When he brought the 'trophy' in to the fraternity the frat brothers were shocked and amazed. It seems they wouldn't go downtown either!"

Kevin continues:

"Mike taught me many things during our time together. Besides self-defense, survival techniques, marksmanship, horseback riding, patriotism, and love of country, he instilled in me a love for and interest in military history and building and collecting military models.

"We frequently had 'wars' with our model soldiers and equipment which proved to be lessons in tactics for me. One evening we were setting up for a contest and he explained a very flexible tactical formation to me and then proceeded to beat the pants off me, as usual. Later, when my interest in

78

Napoleon was blossoming, I realized Mike had shown me the Emperor's Battalion Carre (Battalion Square) from the Jena Campaign. Mike is still with me in a way, for I now have his collection of soldiers and models, which, joined with mine, numbers over 5,000 pieces.

"In many ways he was a very private person and never mentioned some things. When our dad died while Mike was a yearling at West Point, he had a hard time. He didn't come home for the funeral, as my mom urged him not to. So, he stayed at school but didn't tell anyone. My mom received a call from Mike's TAC sometime later asking what was wrong. She explained the situation, as Mike had kept it to himself. The TAC remarked that all Mike had to do was let him know and he would take care of it.

"After our dad died, Mike took over as head of the household. Even though he was away most of the year, he always came home for leave and we looked forward to his arrival. Mike's homecomings were always a major event. Even in the middle of the night I would get up to see him. He was always glad to see me and spent most of his leave with me.

"One time while on leave before his first assignment in Korea we were riding on a streetcar in San Francisco. Two malevolent characters ahead of us paid their bill with a ten and said they gave the conductor a twenty. Mike quickly responded that, no, it was a ten, and proceeded to stare the two down.

"Another time, in a restaurant in San Juan Capistrano, Mike went over to a rude, very loud and abusive, foul-mouthed customer and asked him to be quiet or step outside. The customer became very quiet and as we finished our meal the waitress came over and thanked Mike."

Upon graduation on 3 June 1964 Mike was commissioned in the Armor. That August he was a member of the first "non-volunteer" Ranger class. Mike Moran recalls those times:

"Mike was a cheerleader for our Ranger class and always kept our spirits up. He was a natural leader who never complained and always gave 110 percent. He also possessed the ultimate asset, a large, old, brown DeSoto, which we would pile into for a trip to eat our fill at the Black Angus during our infrequent breaks in training. I remember Mike as a kind young man and try to imagine him at our age now. I can't do that. To me, he will always be the twenty-three-year-old lieutenant who was a true friend and an outstanding officer. He typified our youth, dreams, and idealism. I miss him."

Mike volunteered to go to Korea for his first assignment. Shortly before leaving there he was talking with Bruce Foster who said that after West Point, Airborne and Ranger Schools, plus the "short tour," he had a strong desire to get back to "the World." In late 1965, the growing war in Vietnam was just beginning to draw attention and had just claimed the Class of '64's first two casualties there, David Ugland and Clair Thurston. As a professional soldier, Mike felt compelled to be where the action was. Realizing that it was an infantryman's war, he transferred to the infantry and volunteered for Vietnam where he won a Bronze Star with Valor and an Air Medal (along with several Vietnamese medals) while serving with the First Cavalry Division. He then was assigned to Fort Lewis, Washington, but after only seven months he again volunteered for Vietnam.

Mike was assigned to the 173d Airborne Brigade in the Central Highlands, where a series of border battles with the North Vietnamese Army was being fought. In October 1967 he assumed command of Company A, Second Battalion, 503d Infantry, a unit of veteran infantrymen, which was involved in some of the most vicious combat of the Vietnam War. In a short period of time, Mike was to earn four Silver Stars, the first one being for personally going outside the perimeter, under intense enemy fire, to rescue one of his wounded soldiers. He led by personal example and professional skill throughout his brief tenure as a combat commander.

His last few days typify his life of courage, honor, dedication to duty, and love of his fellow man. Two days before

Mike was killed, during fierce combat near Dak To, he was wounded by a mortar fragment through his knee. He refused to be evacuated, however, and stayed with his company. He did order his executive officer (XO) to the rear, as he had been wounded in the hand and it had become infected. The XO would return several days later to help reorganize the company (twenty-eight survivors of 101).

On 19 November the battalion was committed to assault NVA positions on Hill 875 and began moving up the hill in classic two-up, one-back formation. D Company was on the left, C Company, under Captain Hal Kaufman (Mike's classmate and good friend), was on the right, and A Company brought up the rear. Before long the lead companies came under intense enemy fire, so Mike had his unit set up rear security and prepare a landing zone to evacuate the wounded. Through a series of tunnels and trails, the NVA was able to surround the three companies with superior force. Captain Mike Kiley had just been hit again by mortar shrapnel in the back and was having the wound dressed when he and his command group were overwhelmed and all were killed.

Numerous books have since been written describing what became known as the Battle of Dak To. Mike has figured prominently in seven of them, particularly *The Long Gray Line* and *Dak To*. Many good men died in that campaign and Mike Kiley was among the best of them, if not the best.

His loss has been deeply felt by his family, classmates, and fellow soldiers. Nevertheless, we all recognize that he went to West Point to serve his country as a professional soldier. He did so with distinction and his life was, and continues to be, an example for us all.

Chapter Eleven

Harold James Kaufman

When Hal comes bouncing out of these grey halls, it will be with a hard earned diploma clenched in his rip-cord hand. Skydiving was his amusement and academics, his aversion. Twice a year he faced the test, but his rugged determination, lubricated with midnight oil, carried him through. This trooper will be going up, be it in rank or a C-119.

The battle for Hill 875 had not been going well. Captain Harold Kaufman, the commander of C Company, Second Battalion, 503d Infantry, 173d Airborne Brigade had spent most of the day of 19 November 1967 leading an uphill attack against a well-dug-in, heavily fortified enemy force. His company and D Company, on his left, had already suffered several casualties when shouts of "Friendly! Friendly!" were heard to the rear. The shouts were from a small number of survivors of A Company, which had been bringing up the rear, and were scrambling up the hill to join C and D Companies after having been decimated by the overpowering enemy. Hal quickly found out his classmate and good friend, Mike Kiley, the A Company Commander, had been killed during the attack. Realizing that since they wiped out someone as tough as Mike, and most of his company, Hal quickly calculated that the enemy must be much stronger than what had been anticipated.

Hal organized a tight defensive perimeter with what was left of the three companies. They requested water and ammunition, but in the space of seventy-five minutes, three helicopters were shot down attempting to resupply. Artillery, Air Force jets and C-130 miniguns were supporting them as they prepared to spend the night in place before relief would arrive the following day. At 6:58 P.M. an American fighter bomber passed over the position and dropped two 500-pound bombs. The first landed just outside the perimeter amidst a group of North Vietnamese as they prepared to attack and killed at least twenty-five of them. Unfortunately, and tragically, the second bomb exploded in the middle of the C Company command post, killing forty-two men, including Hal Kaufman. Forty-five others were wounded. This incident of

83

"friendly fire" was one of the most serious of the Vietnam War. Throughout the history of warfare "friendly-fire" casualties have been an inglorious hazard. Even with the advancement of modern weapons technology, mistakes continue to be made. And, it is also very difficult to be perfectly precise. Of all the Class of '64's combat deaths, Hal's was the only one caused by "friendly fire". His was the fifth and last loss for the class in 1967. By the end of the year there would be 500,000 American military personnel in Vietnam—almost double the quantity at the end of 1966.

For the next four days the Americans continued shelling the enemy positions, sending in reinforcements and evacuating the casualties while the NVA's 174th Regiment melted away into Cambodia, only four miles away. Hill 875 was finally taken on Thanksgiving Day, 23 November 1967, at a very high cost. An estimated 248 NVA soldiers had died while United States' losses were 107 killed, 282 wounded and ten missing. Before the tragedy, Hal had already won a Silver Star, two Bronze Stars (one with valor), two Air Medals and a Purple Heart. The losses were felt deeply by many, especially the class of '64, whose two fallen warriors were among the most dedicated, experienced, and capable of all.

Hal came to the class from Spring Valley, New York, only a few miles away from the academy. He was the son of Adelaide and Charles and the younger brother of Charles, Junior. Throughout his youth Hal was perpetually in motion. During the school year it was books and sports, and during the summers it was work. Some of his summer jobs included being a caddy, a construction worker, and a truck driver. Realizing that he wanted to attend West Point and pursue a military career, Hal transferred to Valley Forge Military Academy in Pennsylvania for his last two years of high school in order to maximize his preparation. However, he fell just a whisker short of obtaining an appointment after he graduated in 1959, so he set his sights on 1960. During that year he attended a college board preparation course at Braden's Prep School in

Cornwall-on-Hudson, New York. Several of his future classmates were also there.

I remember Braden's was a large, old ten-or eleven-bedroom house overlooking the Hudson River, about six miles north of West Point. There were two or three wise and seasoned instructors who conducted several courses each year, mostly for service academy aspirants. (Charlie Hutchison and Tom Kerns were in a later course.) Each course had thirty or forty students, crammed three or four to a bedroom. The order of the day was study, study, study. We spent the whole day in the classroom and had a ton of homework every night. Some of us got out and around the local area for some sports and social activities, but not Hal. Since he had barely missed getting into the academy the year before, he wasn't taking any chances this time. Without a doubt, he put in more hours of study than anyone else in our course. He kept a smile on his face, but underneath there was an intense determination. Hal won the admiration of all of us and was an outstanding example of perseverance. It was no surprise when he was awarded an appointment to join the Class of '64 that summer.

As a cadet, Hal was a popular, down-to-earth friend to all. His best buddy was Bill Jackman, who recalls their time together: "Hal and I became best friends during our four years together at West Point. It began with 'Beast Barracks,' as it did for most of us. Hal and I found ourselves in the same company, Third Company, New Cadet Barracks. Alphabetical destiny placed us in the same platoon, squad, and as roommates, the ultimate in cadet kinship. In fact, Hal and I roomed together for three of our four years at West Point. We went to Company G-2 for plebe and yearling years and then ended up in E-2 together for cow and firstie years. Returning to 'Beast Barracks,' Hal was a lifesaver for me in at least two ways. First, he was meticulous, thorough and precise in shining shoes and brass, aligning and folding uniforms, etc., as he had acquired those skills at Valley Forge. Since I knew nothing of such arts, his help was invaluable to a hick straight off the farm and scared out of my wits. Second, he deflected attention from me at drill. Though good at all the technical movements and always in step, Hal 'bounced' as he marched. Thus, the upperclassmen were all over him constantly. He could not help me during parades though, because we were always sized and Hal was a runt. Despite the attention he drew, Hal 'bounced' for four years and was readily identified in any moving formation.

"As we moved into the academic year, I was able to return the favors. Hal was a true goat, with stereotypical goat mentality, i.e., 'Don't sweat it.' In a pattern which was to recur for four years, but which was especially prevalent plebe year, Hal would do the absolute minimum of studying during the semester. He had almost no interest in academics. He would be failing a course for most of the semester and then decide two or three days before the exam that it was time to study. That meant I had to tutor him, especially in math and Portuguese, but also in other subjects as the years went by. So we would 'cram' together until one or two in the morning, putting up the blankets over the windows after taps, even though I wanted to sleep and arrive at the exams rested. Trying to pound academic concepts into Hal was sheer torture, but we both persevered. Several times he was too deficient to make it all up and had to take the turnout exams. This represented another two weeks of hell for both of us, but he always made it.

"Near the end of plebe year, Hal found his true love, the Cadet Parachute Club. Every free/waking moment from then on, Hal would spend on this activity. As the club's president during firstie year, he helped it achieve the prominence it enjoys today. By the time he graduated he had close to 300 jumps. The Parachute Club must have been an unlucky place for our classmates, however. Besides Hal, four other club members from our class would die in Vietnam, KB Kindleberger, Marty Green, Bob Walters, and Johnny Graham. Rooming together our final semester, Hal was always at

86

Stewart Air Force Base jumping. The only time he spent in the barracks was when bad weather precluded jumping. At those times, he spent hours at the heavy-duty sewing machine he had brought into our room, repairing club parachutes."

With his adventurous spirit, action-oriented Hal didn't surprise anyone when he chose the infantry as his branch.

As was the norm for the class, he attended the Airborne and Ranger courses in the fall of 1964. Needless to say, Hal laughed his way through the former. Those five jumps were probably the easiest he ever made! Ranger School was more demanding (to say the least) but Hal earned his tab and reported to the First Battalion, Thirty-first Infantry, in Korea in December. Thirteen months later, declining the guaranteed follow-on assignment in the Continental United States, he volunteered for duty in Vietnam and attended the Military Assistance Training Advisory Course at Fort Bragg, North Carolina. Hal then attended an intensive twelve-week Vietnamese language course at the Defense Language Institute in Monterey, California, in order to complete his preparation to work directly with the South Vietnamese Army.

He arrived in Vietnam in May 1966 and served a full year as assistant battalion advisor to the Fifth Vietnamese Airborne Battalion. Hal enjoyed the assignment and was impressed with the professionalism of the Vietnamese airborne soldiers. Some Vietnamese military units did not have very good reputations, but their airborne and ranger units were highly capable, dedicated and tough. After that year, Hal could have returned to the States but his warrior instinct led him to volunteer for an extension in country. So, he went home for a month of leave and returned to Vietnam for the assignment every young combat arms officer wants—company commander in combat.

Hal had been the commander of C Company for almost five months of successful combat operations and only had a little more than a month remaining of his tour when his last campaign began.

In late October 1967 Army Intelligence estimated that Dak To, in the Central Highlands, was threatened by six NVA regiments and a Viet Cong battalion. On 1 November the 173d was airlifted by C-130's to the area and commenced Operation MacArthur, frequently making contact with the enemy. On 18 November a Special Forces unit encountered the enemy entrenched on the top of Hill 875, twelve miles southwest of Dak To. After two brief firefights, the SF team withdrew with ten wounded. The next day, after an artillery and bomb preparation, the Second Battalion, 503d Infantry moved out to take Hill 875. Almost immediately the Sky Soldiers ran into a blistering wall of small-arms, automatic weapons, rocket and grenade fire from the well-dug-in enemy. Hal requested additional artillery and close air support and then continued the uphill attack. The advance stalled, however, as the enemy pinned down the attackers from the rear. That dreadful day, Captains Mike Kiley and Hal Kaufman became the tenth and eleventh combat victims of the class. How ironic that it was the second time that two members of the class were killed the same day, in the same battle, each time with the 173d! Those four deaths, David, Clair, Mike, and Hal represent the most the Class of '64 suffered in any brigade-size organization. It was just bad luck, for the 173d was an outstanding unit with outstanding soldiers. It only existed for nine years, though, as it was deactivated on 14 January 1972 as part of the reduction of American Forces in Vietnam.

Many men aspire to the life of a true adventurer. Hal was one. From his first jump to the last time he went up Hill 875, he sought and thrived on a life of action. In so doing he was a noble example of devotion to duty and to country. His desire to lead men in combat was not just a result of what an infantry officer is supposed to want; it was a true reflection of Harold Kaufman. He died leading the life he loved—being a good soldier.

Bill Jackman closes: "Two months after graduation Hal served as an usher at my wedding, the last time I was to see him. I often visit him now at Arlington National Cemetery and reflect on our memories—young cadets and junior officers, frozen in time."

Chapter Twelve

Charles Kirby Wilcox

From the neighborhood of the riverboat gamblers, Kirby has upheld their tradition with constant card games and numerous ideas for "money making" business schemes. "Fluent" French and a mile-long line conquered almost all the women he met. Enthusiasm and clear thinking spelled success for Kirby at the Academy and will do the same after graduation.

The year 1968 was America's busiest in Vietnam. Our troop strength would rise to approximately 540,000 early in the year and would stay at that level until early the following year when we started to wind down our efforts. On the ninth day of 1968 the Class of '64 lost its twelfth warrior, Charles Kirby Wilcox, an All-American young man from the heartland. Like Denis Galloway, he was from Missouri, and was extremely proud of his beloved home state.

At the time of Kirby's death most Americans believed we had the upper hand in Vietnam, which we did, despite a growing amount of protest. That attitude changed dramatically, however, a short time later when the Tet Offensive began on the 30th of January. As had been customary, a truce was agreed upon to commence that day, the beginning of the lunar new year, so that both sides could celebrate with their families. At dawn the North Vietnamese Army and the Viet Cong coordinated a massive attack on South Vietnam's seven largest cities and on thirty provincial capitals ranging from the Delta to the DMZ (the demilitarized zone between North and South Vietnam). For the most part, the defenders of South Vietnam were caught by surprise. Hanoi fully expected to topple South Vietnam with such an all-out effort, but by the tenth of February had suffered a crushing military defeat with over 50,000 killed and hundreds of thousands wounded. Despite the fact that Tet was a significant military victory for the United States and South Vietnam, it turned out to be a disaster for us, psychologically and politically. The enemy's ability to achieve the element of surprise on such a large scale was exploited by the media and the American public became convinced that the war was unwinnable. Even though we continued to make military progress against a weakened enemy, domestic pres-

91

sure prevailed and our government decided that enough was enough. President Johnson decided not to run for re-election and then later, his successor, Richard Nixon, started bringing the troops home.

Kirby was born on 4 June 1942 in Springfield, Missouri, the son of Betty and Charlie Wilcox. His younger sister, Patti, came along three years later. Father Charlie was not a career military man but he was a veteran of World War II. As a boy Kirby was active in scouting and was a standout Little League baseball player. At Parkview High School he was known as an all-around athlete, an excellent student, and a model citizen. He lettered in both baseball and football and was the captain of the Parkview American Legion baseball team when it won the state championship.

By the time he finished high school, Kirby had received athletic scholarship offers from the University of Southern California, Arizona State University, and the University of Arizona. He was also offered an academic scholarship to the University of Missouri. But, quite early in life Kirby had expressed a desire to attend West Point and become an army officer. So, when he received a principal appointment from Representative Charles Brown of Missouri's Seventh Congressional District, he disdained those other offers and headed for the Military Academy to join the Class of '64.

The transition to cadet life was no problem for Kirby, although like most of his classmates who hadn't had a military background, he found the "Beast Barracks" experience to be a rude introduction to his new world. One of the most dreaded events that occasionally took place during that summer of 1960 was the clothing formation. The first of those formations started out with Kirby and the other new plebes standing in a company formation, awaiting instructions from the company commander while being harassed by the rest of the cadre. Dressed in fatigues and combat boots, they were expecting to be marched off to a lecture when the commander's voice echoed through their ranks, "SMACKHEADS, IT IS NOW 1400

HOURS. YOU HAVE EXACTLY FIVE MINUTES TO BE BACK IN THIS FORMATION IN DRESS GRAY OVER WHITE, UNDERARMS. NOW, MOVE OUT!" As he ran back to his room, Kirby almost couldn't believe that he was going to have to completely change his uniform. Clothes flew all around the room as Kirby and his roommates rushed into the new outfit, grabbed their rifles, and ran back outside where the upperclassmen descended upon them for a frenzied inspection of their new attire. The latecomers were herded into a separate group and berated unmercifully. Once again, the company commander's voice bellowed, "THAT WAS A GROSS PERFORMANCE, YOU DULLARDS. IT IS NOW 1410 HOURS. BE BACK HERE BY 1415 IN GYM A UNDER RAINCOAT. MOVE OUT!"

This game continued for almost an hour. By then the new cadets had exhaustively donned every type of clothing combination possible and were dripping with sweat. The conditioning hike that followed was a welcome relief. Even the stressful nightly shower formations seemed tame compared to clothing formations. However, it was one way to learn what each of the many uniforms entailed. And, it was another of many drills designed to teach the new cadets how to function under pressure.

Kirby had always been able to perform well under pressure, and at the academy he was well known for his calm and efficient approach in overcoming the many obstacles that each cadet faced during the four years. He took academics in stride and found time for numerous extracurricular activities. During plebe year he played baseball but gave it up for the last three years in favor of intramural athletics. Kirby was chosen the Most Valuable Intramural Athlete during his first-class year, and enjoyed the dubious honor of being cadet-in-charge of the Goat-Engineer Football Game. This is an annual event that precedes the Army-Navy game, which Army is supposed to win if the team of academic goats is victorious. The Engineer (hives) team must have won that year.

He was a member of the Debate Council and Forum all four years and served as chairman of the National Debate Tournament during his last year. Twelve of the twenty-four fallen warriors of the class had participated in the Debate Council and Forum. Since its membership was not that large, such a statistic would place it in the same unlucky category as the Parachute Club.

Although French was his weakest subject, that didn't stop Kirby from being a four-year member of the French Club. During his first-class year he also was selected to be a Rabble-rouser, an Army cheerleader. The selection criteria were the same as for cheerleaders anywhere else: good looks, enthusiasm, popularity, and athleticism. It is little wonder that Kirby was chosen to be the activities officer on the brigade staff during his last year.

June of 1964 brought graduation, and Kirby returned to Springfield to marry his sweetheart, Linda Lou Hanks. In August he reported to Fort Benning for Ranger and Airborne Schools, after which he was assigned to the Second Infantry Division in Korea for a year. While there he served as an infantry platoon leader and as aide to Brigadier General Gleszer (the father of classmate Pete Gleszer), who was then assistant division commander of the division. Upon his return from Korea in December 1965, Kirby attended the Maintenance Officer's Course at Fort Knox, Kentucky, for twelve weeks. He and Linda then went to Baumholder, Germany, where he joined the First Battalion, Thirteenth Infantry, of the Eighth Infantry Division. Because of the ongoing build-up of U.S. Forces in Vietnam at that time, the army units in Germany were extremely short on personnel, especially officers. As a consequence, during his sixteen months in the 1/13th, Kirby saw duty as a platoon leader, company commander, battalion S-3 and battalion executive officer. The latter two jobs were positions for majors and Kirby filled them as a brand-new captain!

Despite the job challenges and seasoning that Kirby was experiencing, he knew that Germany was not where he should be in 1967. His country and his classmates and other comrades in arms were getting more heavily involved in the conflict in Southeast Asia and several of his good friends had already died trying to stem the Communist advances in South Vietnam. Kirby could not avoid doing his part—it was what he, as an American fighting man, should do. Besides, in less than three years in the army he had already done everything possible, and more. There was only one thing lacking—combat participation. So, that spring he volunteered for duty in Vietnam.

On 7 June 1967 Linda and Kirby were blessed with a son, Curtis Scott, whose arrival made both parents extremely proud and happy. A short time later they were all on their way back to Springfield, Missouri, where Kirby settled his little family and went on to Vietnam. Young Curt was seven weeks old.

In Vietnam Kirby was initially assigned as a staff officer in the First Cavalry Division's Support Command. In his letters he expressed a dislike for his support duties, even though he knew that his job was a necessary one and that it was customary practice to spend time in the rear while earning the privilege of commanding a company. Occasionally he would see his old pal from the Cadet Brigade Staff, Mike Nawrosky (Chapter 14), who was already commanding a company in the division, and feel twinges of envy. Larry Brewer, who was flying helicopters in support of the First Cav at that time and saw Kirby often, recalls how anxious he was to get out of the paperwork and into the action. Finally, after five months in the rear, Kirby got his wish and assumed command of an infantry company. As an infantry officer, there was nothing more important than combat command, and Kirby was ready for it, mentally and physically. As fate would have it, however, after only two weeks on the job, the young captain was felled by an enemy grenade while leading his company on a search and destroy mission near Bong San.

It was another tragic loss—for his family, his country, and his class. In everything that he ever attempted during his short twenty-five-year life, Kirby excelled. His performance always drew praise and admiration. Whatever the task, Kirby could be counted on to give it everything he had—and that is just what he did on the 9th day of January 1968.

Kirby was buried at the National Cemetery in Springfield, Missouri, on 18 January 1968 following a military funeral. Classmate Jim Mozden (who would die of cancer five years later) served as escort officer, and Jay Bennett, Bob Hillyer, Mike Moran, Marty Ischinger, Bill Kelley, and Mike Liebowitz served as pallbearers.

One of Kirby's many close friends in the class was class president, Dick Chilcoat. They had been roommates yearling year in F-1 and were reunited on the brigade staff firstie year— Dick was the brigade commander. (As expected, Dick rose to "star" level in the army. At the time of this writing he was a major general and the commandant of the Army War College.) He later reflected on Kirby: "He had accomplished much in the few years given him to spend on earth. He was a great son...and older brother. His athletic prowess was obvious at all levels, as was his scholarship and citizenship. And at the academy, his cadetship, leadership, and friendship were valued as much as precious gold...he was a classmate extraordinaire. Upon graduation, he continued to excel as officer, as husband, and as father.

"He personified the themes espoused in Rudyard Kipling's immortal poem, *If*, which, in a few short verses, captured the essence of what it takes to be a man. The last verses seem especially relevant in Kirby's case:

> If you can talk with crowds and keep your virtue,
> Or walk with Kings - nor lose the common touch.
> If neither foes nor loving friends can hurt you,
> If all men count with you, but none too much;

If you can fill the unforgiving minute
With sixty seconds' worth of distance run,
Yours is the earth and everything that's in it,
And - which is more - you'll be a man, my son!

"In some twenty-five years, Kirby Wilcox had filled '... the unforgiving minute with sixty seconds' worth of distance run...' and he was '...a man, my son!' He earned and possessed the personal and professional love of all who ever knew him...and, thus, he made history in his own time because he touched our very souls and the depths of our hearts. And he endures."

Years later Linda married Keith Lindsay and the two of them enjoyed the pleasure of raising Curt. Curt graduated from the University of Kansas with a business degree and later earned a masters in finance from the University of Missouri. Like his father, he has excelled in everything and is presently running the family business. He is also a happy husband and the proud father of Kirby's grandson, Ryan Scott. What a proud grandfather Kirby would be!

These pictures depict the three principal staffs of the Corps of Cadets from September 1963 to June 1964.

The Brigade Staff had six members including:

Kirby Wilcox (Chapter 12)

Mike Nawrosky (Chapter 14)

There were five cadets on each Regimental Staff:

First Regiment:

Cliff McKittrick (Chapter 8)

Second Regiment:

Bob Serio (Chapter 13)

KB Kindleberger (Chapter 4)

It must be considered an almost incredible statistic that thirty-one percent (five of sixteen) of these key class leaders would fall in combat—all in Vietnam. Overall, four percent of the Class of '64 died in combat.

BRIGADE STAFF

Kirby Wilcox, Activities Officer—*Chapter 12*
Mike Nawrosky, Adjutant—*Chapter 14*
Denny Culp, Executive Officer
Dick Chilcoat, Brigade Commander
Tony Hartle, Operations Officer
Bill Reynolds, Supply Officer

FIRST REGIMENTAL STAFF

Jere Richardson, Operations Officer
Cliff McKittrick, Executive Officer—*Chapter 8*
Norm Grunstad, Regimental Commander
Wayne Wheeler, Adjutant
Bob Michela, Supply Officer

SECOND REGIMENTAL STAFF

Bob Serio, Adjutant—*Chapter 13*
Jim Gantsoudes, Executive Officer
K. B. Kindleberger, Regimental Commander—*Chapter 4*
John Kyle, Training Officer
Don Renfro, Supply Officer

Chapter Thirteen

Robert Frank Serio

On the first day, Bob thought he heard from the Poop deck, "Italians, RISE!" He did not cease to work on that command for four years. His positive and aggressive nature and his genuine ability are reflected in everything he touches. You can disagree with the man but you can neither deny him nor refute him.

A nother couple who suffered the tragedy of losing their only child was Janette and Bob Serio, whose son, Bob, or Bobby, as he was usually called, was mortally wounded on 17 April 1968 during the Tet counteroffensive in Vietnam. That was just a little over three months after Kirby Wilcox's death and a little less than three months before Mike Nawrosky's.

Young Bobby was born and raised in the Bronx where he attended the first six grades at P.S. 21 and the last six at Mount Saint Michael. His mother reports that, as a youngster, he was a typical boy with lots of friends and all the same loveable traits and also the shortcomings that all people possess. In high school he really began to bloom academically and athletically, as he won numerous trophies with the debating team and the track and field team. At one of the track meets, his team's javelin thrower was sick, and so as not to forfeit the event, the coach asked Bob to fill in. He did so and took the first place trophy.

Bob was the valedictorian of his high school graduating class of over 300 students. He received several college scholarship offers but turned them all down—his only desire was to attend West Point. In the Extempore Speech contest held in Washington, D.C., in 1959 Bob placed third in the nation. His ability to think on his feet was again evident a few years later when he was a member of the prestigious Debate Council and Forum at the Military Academy.

Not having any brothers or sisters to grow up with, Bob became very close to his cousins in the neighborhood. Rita Caldararo, five years older than Bob, remembers him as a smart and beautiful little boy with gorgeous curly hair. At eight months of age he could recite his first and last names. Although he was an only child, he was not spoiled, he was a regular guy who was easy to talk to and had a great sense of humor. One Thanksgiving the entire family got together at the famous restaurant, Mama Leone's, where the doorman was dressed as a pilgrim for the occasion. When one of the aunts commented that the doorman must have been an Italian peasant since it was an Italian restaurant, Rita recalls that she and Bob almost died laughing and she frequently reminisces about that moment. She also fondly remembers her many visits with her husband and children to West Point during Bob's cadet days, including the day he entered and the day he graduated. She was often pregnant during those visits, and Bob had to help push her up the hills as they walked from place to place. She said, "When I had my fifth child, Bobby told me I went from a skinny kid to the strongest one in the family." Later Rita was to lament, "Bobby was taken away from us too early. He would have succeeded in anything he would have pursued in life."

Ken Tirella and Bob were very close in age and very close in almost everything they did while growing up. Fun was their first priority as they engaged in sports, fishing, crabbing, Lionel trains, and dating. They spent their hot summer vacations playing stickball, swimming, or just sitting around on the corner talking and playing cards. Bob and Ken also worked together in a supermarket where they shared lots of laughs and fun. They both were pranksters. One year when Bob came home for Christmas from West Point, Ken greeted him with a very short, cadet-type haircut. Bob countered by surprising him with a large, beautifully wrapped Christmas gift. Ken almost fell over when he opened it and found a long blonde wig inside.

The two cousins would often go up to West Point on weekends to see the parades and football games. Ken nostalgically reflects on Bob: "He felt the need and pride to serve his country. Just before he was to leave for Vietnam he came to visit us at our apartment. We had a son then. I didn't know this would be our last time together. Till this day I still have an empty bottle in my refrigerator in which we mixed a couple of drinks. When news of Bobby's death came I can't express the sorrow I felt—also the sorrow for my aunt and uncle who raised such a great son that anyone would be proud of."

As a cadet Bob excelled in every area. "Beast Barracks" was a challenge which he readily accepted, but he was shocked at the vast difference in his new life as a plebe and his old life just a few miles down the road. In fact, the thought often occurred to him that it would be very easy to hop on one of the many trains that passed through the academy grounds and be home in less than an hour. But, as with the other New Yorkers, it was only a thought. After the first skimpy meal on 5 July 1960 the command "Battalions rise!" was given. For the longest time Bob was convinced that the command was "Italians rise!" He didn't encounter many problems at West Point, though, and by the time graduation arrived he was a cadet captain, the adjutant of the second regiment, and was ranked thirty-fourth in the class. Bob was also a stalwart of the Debate Council and Forum and the Rugby Club. Rugby teammate Bill Jackman said, "While I was a grubby 'scrumdog,' Bobby played on the 3/4 line, the handsome running back who scored all the points, never got dirty and won all the girls. ... This image fit Bobby to a 'T,' though he was never vain about it, and his natural leadership skills showed themselves on the rugby pitch just as they did as a cadet and officer."

Another good friend of Bob's in the class was fellow Bronxite, Art Kelly. The two would often ride home together as their parents took turns doing the driving. Both were bright and strong-willed and frequently engaged in deep-heated discussions about religion, the army, and other areas of contention. However, if the two of them were facing the rest of the world, LOOK OUT! Art cites an example: "Since we both validated Plebe English we ended up in the same section of

105

advanced English that year. We were in class one day discussing some heroic tale from literature—something to do with the forces of good and evil and man's attempt to overcome the dark side. Bob and I got into a HEATED argument with some of our classmates (remember, we both had strong New York accents at the time) and finally the instructor called the whole group to attention by screaming, 'GENTLEMEN!' He then looked at Bob and me and said, 'I can just see you two in a bar in the Bronx with broken bottles in your hands—this is not the way to do this.' Bob and I had many a chuckle over that—since it had been obvious to us that the other guys were all wrong and, of course, since they would not listen to calm reason the answer was to 'go at it.' (Of course, we were plebes and our training had not yet taken.)"

About eight years later, a few months after Bob's death, Art and his wife, Michele, were at West Point visiting Art's brother who later graduated in 1970. Art recalls the event: "As Michele, my brother, and I were walking along Thayer Road we met Bob's folks and a young lady. Now I knew that prior to going to Vietnam he had been engaged but had not wanted to be married until he returned. I also understood that she had wanted to be married before he left. (Keep that in mind as the story unfolds.) His folks were glad to see me, as I was to see them. They introduced us to his fiancee and I introduced them to my wife and brother. After the usual pleasantries they told me that they had just come from visiting Bob's grave. Then it hit me. 'I was not an only child—here was my six-foot-two brother in his gray uniform standing there as they—his parents who had no other children—asked me how my folks were.' And an even worse thought was that I already had had one son before I left for Vietnam and here was his fiancee who would never have his children. What would it have mattered if it had been me instead of him who had not come home? What a sense of loss and waste rolled over me. It was all I could do to finish the conversation. That was the last time I saw his folks but I have never forgotten that meeting."

After graduation Bob spent part of his 1964 summer on the beach in Ocean City, New Jersey. Steve Weisel was there too, and provided the following: "There were about six of us from the class who rented a beach house for a month. Needless to say, after our four years of semi-confinement, we had a blast. What I remember most is that Bob Serio was the unquestionable leader of the group. I hadn't known him very well as a cadet, but in that short amount of time it was clear that he was a natural leader. He didn't scream and boss people around—he just had an awareness, a calmness, and a knack of taking charge. The rest of us looked up to him with admiration and respect. There was no doubt in any of our minds that Bob would reach the highest levels of army leadership. It's a real shame that he never got the opportunity."

Bob's first career assignment was in Germany with the Third Battalion, Thirty-second Armor of the Third Armored Division. From there he attended the Tank Leaders Course at the Armor School, after which he assumed command of Company A, First Battalion, Sixty-third Armor at Fort Riley, Kansas. Another company commander in the unit was old rugby buddy, Bill Jackman, who recalls: "Bobby and I became much closer in early 1967 when we both found ourselves, fresh-faced captains, commanding companies in the 1/63 Armor. The Big Red One (First Infantry Division) had already deployed to Vietnam and our tank battalion was to follow later. But first we had to receive the brand-new M551 Sheridan (a light tank)...and conduct the final troop test on it prior to our unit deployment. We had the entire post virtually to ourselves. Bobby and I had a friendly rivalry as to which one of our two companies was the best in the battalion. Luckily, it was one of his Sheridans which sank during a river-crossing so I could haze him unmercifully. Despite a positive article which Bobby wrote for *Armor* magazine, the Sheridan was declared not ready for combat (it later found a home in the Eighty-second

Airborne Division), our battalion was taken off the deployment list and our soldiers were 'levied' to go to Vietnam as
individual replacements. Bobby and I clamored to be released
from the battalion so we could get to Vietnam. I left Fort Riley
in August and never saw Bobby again. He left later and was
killed approximately one month after arrival in Vietnam. Our
old unit escorted his remains from arrival in California to
burial.

"Bobby had that star quality about him, of which I am
reminded every time I visit his grave at West Point. It also
brings into very personal and direct focus words I have heard
from World War I, World War II, and Korean War veterans:
'War is an indiscriminate killer and we are nothing more than
fortunate survivors.' "

In June 1978 at Fort Knox, Kentucky, Colonel Thomas W.
Kelly, the 194th Armored Brigade Commander, made the following remarks as he conducted the ceremony dedicating
Serio Hall and Serio Park (Bob had been then Major Kelly's
assistant operations officer before taking command of A Troop,
First Squadron, Fourth Cavalry five days before his death):
"We name this building today to honor a superb young
man...but in a larger sense to honor all our fallen comrades
from all our wars. ... I was with him then and had given him
the order that committed his troops to the battle. An aero
rifle infantry platoon had been inserted into a patch of jungle
along a rice paddy. ... Immediately upon debarking the aircraft, the infantry was ambushed and received a withering
fire causing heavy casualties, pinning them down. ... Without
relief they would have been annihilated. ... Captain Serio immediately rallied his forces and moved them ten miles to the
location of the friendly infantry unit, where his unit was confronted by the enemy's devastating fire. With complete dis-
regard for his personal safety, Captain Serio positioned his
vehicle at the point of contact where he could best control the
action of his elements. He personally directed each vehicle
into a strategic position between the pinned-down infantry

unit and the enemy force, and chose a secured landing zone to be utilized by helicopters evacuating the wounded. After securing the friendly forces' positions, he assigned each platoon a sector of fire and began an attack which routed the enemy from their bunkers and entrenched positions, thus saving the lives of his brothers in the infantry. As the enemy broke contact, his track received a direct hit from an enemy rocket-propelled grenade and Captain Serio was mortally wounded. For his valor in this close combat against numerically superior hostile forces, he was awarded the Silver Star, posthumously. 'Greater love hath no man than he lay down his life for the life of a friend.'

"I was then, as I am now, convinced that Bob Serio would have risen to the very highest levels of the military and he was my personal choice for future chief of staff of the army. ... Those of us who knew, respected, and loved Bob will always remember him as a tower of strength and a shining example to be emulated, but more importantly, he touched us and we knew he passed our way."

Chapter Fourteen

Michael Robert Nawrosky

After a year at Colgate, Mike came to West Point with stars in his eyes and his sights set on a military career. After several losing bouts with the surgeon's blade ended Mike's athletic career, he found coaching the Plebe 150's a satisfying challenge.

As the command "PASS IN REVIEW!" echoed across the plain at West Point, the twenty-four companies of cadets, 2,400 strong, began their sub-commands and maneuvers. The G.A.P. (cadets referred to the spectators as the G.A.P.—Great American Public) encircling the plain watched in awe as the precision marching unfolded and the Corps of Cadets passed by the reviewing stand and disappeared into the barracks areas.

It was the spring of 1964 and the booming voice giving the commands belonged to Cadet Michael R. Nawrosky, the brigade adjutant. Some of the spectators may have thought that the cadet with the loudest voice automatically was selected to be the brigade adjutant. However, the selection process is much more intricate. In fact, the brigade adjutant must be one of the highest rated cadets in his class, probably in the top five percent in military aptitude, as rated by his peers and superiors. A strong voice is an added plus. Mike Nawrosky was the whole package—highly rated and in possession of a resounding command voice.

Mike came from Dumont, New Jersey, the son of hardworking, second generation American parents, Mary and Michael, whose lives were centered around their two children, Mike and his younger sister (by six years), Marilyn. As a high school student-athlete he was known as "Dumont's answer to Jim Thorpe." In addition to earning three varsity letters, he was the quarterback and co-captain of the football team as well as co-captain of the track team, on which he excelled in the dashes, broad jump, shot put, and discus. Not only was Mike an outstanding athlete, he was also an outstanding student and leader. He was the president of the National Honor Society, and a member of the high school paper staff, the

111

Spiked Shoe Club, and the Engineering and Science Club. In Boys State he participated as "Mayor" and "Senator." To cap things off he was voted "Best All-Round Senior Male" at Dumont High School.

He desperately wanted to go to West Point and had all the qualifications. However, since there was so much competition for academy appointments in New Jersey, due to its proximity, Mike was not able to secure an appointment for 1959 when he graduated from high school. So he attended Colgate University in upstate New York for a year and then joined the USMA Class of 1964 on 5 July 1960. Mike did not enjoy "Beast Barracks"—no one ever does—but he seemed to handle it better than most. It undoubtedly had something to do with his personal motivation, high intelligence, superb strength, and athletic ability. As a plebe, Mike excelled in all areas and at the close of the year he received the Association of Graduates' annual award for outstanding military efficiency and leadership. The only setback he encountered was knee surgery which ended his athletic career and relegated him to coaching status—of the plebe 150-pound football team.

Mike continued to shine as an upperclassman, both in the classroom and out, where he was a member of the Rocket Society, Russian Club, Dialectic Society, and Glee Club. In fact, Mike was a paragon of military bearing, integrity, and competence, so much so, that those who didn't know him well tended to consider him rigid, too "gray hog" (gung-ho), or too straight. But those who knew him well knew of his warm heart and rock-solid loyalty. Labor Day weekend, 1963, serves as evidence.

Mike and several other classmates spent that last weekend before their final year of academics at my family's summer lake house in New Jersey, partying, boating, and playing sports. The morning of the day of departure, Labor Day, Mike, Carl Dye, my sister, Mary Lynn, and I went to play tennis, leaving behind two other classmates who shall remain unnamed. When we returned to the house at about noon, we found two extremely inebriated classmates on the front porch who tried to explain that they thought it would be a good idea not to waste any of the liquor left over in the several bottles from the previous night's party. Not a drop was wasted—and from the condition of the two revelers, a lot of drops must have remained in those four or five bottles. Within a short period of time, each of the two exhibited a different type of intoxication—one passed out and the other practically went berserk.

Mike and the rest of us now had a challenging mission: To get our drunken friends dressed properly (coat and tie) and safely returned to their rooms in the barracks, a one-and-a-half-hour drive away. Dressing one was not a problem—it was like dressing a corpse. The real problem was the other one. Before being dressed, he had to be caught and held down. In the meantime, he was running amok through the neighborhood, and at one point he tackled a young lady (who had attended the party the night before) into the lake. It took the efforts of all four of us to hold down our energized friend and get him dressed. Almost dressed, that is, because it was impossible to put his socks on due to his constant thrashing. Next, the car had to be loaded in a manner that would ensure the safety of all six during the trip. After a careful assessment of various possible courses of action, we decided to put Carl and me in the backseat with the wild one between us. That way, we could restrain him so that he couldn't open a door or harass the driver, Mary Lynn. Mike sat between Mary Lynn and the "corpse," as a final line of defense from backseat attacks, and to assist his classmate on his right. The arrangement worked well as the two rear bodyguards were able to constrain all outbursts, and Mike was able to protect the driver and help the heap on his right keep his head steady as he hung it out the window to eliminate some of the poison he had imbibed.

Upon arrival at the North Area sally port by the gymnasium, we faced the last portion of the mission—to cross

113

through North Area and part of Central Area without being detected by any officers, and tuck the two drunks in their beds to sleep it off for an hour before supper formation. As Mike half carried the "corpse," Carl and I had our hands full trying to control the "jack-in-the-box," who was in the final throes of his drunken frenzy. Miraculously, we arrived undetected at our destination and the two party boys were soon snoring. Stories abound of some cadets in high positions who turn in contemporaries for misbehavior. Mike Nawrosky certainly could have cited his two classmates for their gross performance, but all he thought about was lending them a hand—a sincere gesture of flexibility and loyalty.

It was no surprise to anyone when Mike chose the infantry branch when the class made their selections in February of 1964. After graduating one hundred twenty-first in the class on 3 June, Mike served as best man at the wedding of his classmate and good friend, Jay Cope, and his bride, Peggy. He then spent the next sixty days of graduation leave zipping around the countryside in his red Corvette. Occasionally, he took his mother and sister for rides, a thrill they hadn't been accustomed to. In August Mike reported to Fort Benning, the "Home of the Infantry," where he breezed through Airborne School and then attended Ranger School, commonly known as the toughest school in the army. It was even tough for Mike, but he still completed the course in November as the honor graduate, once again exhibiting his ability to excel under the most difficult circumstances.

Mike's first assignment was a thirteen-month tour in Korea, during which time he earned the Army Commendation Medal for "exceptionally meritorious service" as a rifle platoon leader and the battalion 4.2-inch heavy-mortar platoon leader. Seventeen-year-old Marilyn was most happy to maintain her brother's Corvette during his absence. She did have to relinquish it, however, upon Mike's return to the States where he was assigned as aide-de-camp to the commandant of cadets at West Point, a job traditionally offered only to the army's most outstanding lieutenants. It was a most enjoyable time for Mike, working at his alma mater and being near his family. He had the best of both worlds.

Shortly after being promoted to captain, Mike volunteered for duty in Vietnam in an effort to do his part in the service of his country and the free world. During his first nine months there as a company commander in the First Cavalry Division he lost only three men. Then, in April 1968, the First Cav participated in Operation Pegasus, the relief of the besieged American marines at Khe Sanh, an isolated outpost near the North Vietnamese border. Approximately 6,000 marines had been trapped there for over two months, enduring constant shelling and enemy attacks while suffering 256 KIA's and many more wounded. Estimates claim that the enemy's casualties numbered around 10,000. The marines lost an additional fifty-one and the army forty-six during Operation Pegasus, which was successfully completed on April 15th. Among the hundreds wounded was Mike Nawrosky, who suffered shrapnel wounds in the neck while trying to aid an injured comrade. Of all the irony, Mike was unable to speak, but he continued to lead his men by writing his orders on paper. He was later evacuated to Walter Reed Army Medical Center in Washington, D.C., for surgery to restore his voice. Several operations would be required to remove the many pieces of shrapnel and repair his damaged vocal chords. Mike knew that the procedure would be relatively risky, but he had faith and confidence that everything would work out and he would get his voice back.

Unfortunately, though, it didn't work out for Mike as he died on 6 July 1968 after one of the operations. It was less than three months after Bob Serio's death and less than six months after that of Kirby Wilcox. Mike had known both of them very well. He and Bob had shared the adjutant link as firsties—brigade adjutant and regimental adjutant. He and Kirby were on the brigade staff together during firstie year and are pictured side by side in the brigade staff photo (in

115

this book). Mike and Kirby had also seen each other a few times as company commanders together in the First Cav before Kirby was killed. Mike's death made Company G-2 the first company to lose three members of the Class of '64. (He spent his first two years in G-2, along with Charlie Hutchison and Hal Kaufman.) Three other 1960 - 1962 companies would also suffer triple hits among the class, K-1, M-1, and E-2. After the company switch, only Company L-2 would suffer three losses. How unlucky were Charlie Hutchison (G-2 and L-2) and David Ugland (M-1 and K-1)! And David was also a member of that hard-luck "Beast Barracks" squad that lost three of the class's finest!

Mike had frequent visitors while he was in the hospital. One of the last men in the class to see him there before he passed away was Carl Dye, who recalls the encounter: "My wife and I had taken our nine-month-old son, Bill, to Walter Reed for tests for his heart. As we were strolling down a hallway we bumped into Mike, who was cruising along in a wheelchair. Although he had a trache tube in his throat, he seemed to be in good spirits and already had his voice partially restored because he was able to explain to us what was going on, in a low, raspy voice, aided by a voice box. He always had a raspy voice anyway, only before it boomed a lot louder. It was great to see him but then I was shocked and saddened to find out less than a week later that he had died."

Bill Murdy, another close friend of Mike's, remembers the last time he saw Mike: "My wife, Mary, and I were living at Fort Belvoir, Virginia, as I was attending the Engineer Officer Advanced Course. We had invited several people over for a Fourth of July feast, and, as I recall, Jay Cope brought Mike over from Walter Reed. Despite his discomfort, he was able to communicate and was optimistic about his prospects. Mike and I had shared the same 'plebe pop' (officer sponsor) at West Point as well as being in D-2 together during cow year. I had also had the pleasure of accompanying him home to Dumont to spend a weekend with his family. It was a severe blow to

116

me when I learned that he died in the recovery room two days after being in our house. It was a great loss, not only for his family and our class, but also for our army and our nation."

Several months later Mike's parents were posthumously awarded their son's Silver Star and Purple Heart in ceremonies conducted at Fort Monmouth, New Jersey. He had already won a Bronze Star and several Vietnamese medals. In February 1969 the Michael Nawrosky Scholarship Fund was established at Dumont High School by the residents of Dumont, New Jersey.

Mike's sincerity, compassion, love of country, devotion to duty, zest for living, and infectious grin made him very special to all whose lives he enriched with his friendship. Those who knew him best loved him most.

Mike is buried in the cemetery at West Point, where he served so well as a cadet and as an officer.

Chapter Fifteen

Akos Dezso Szekely

Hailing from Hungary, Akos is characterized by a fierce pride and a strong determination. The sports world knows him as a national walking champion. The Academic Department recognized him a four year Star man, but we all know him as a humorous, amiable friend. His boundless ambition and perseverance make him a sure success in his future career.

Nine weeks after Mike Nawrosky died from his wounds, the fifteenth warrior of the Class of '64 fell in combat.

On 28 September 1968 the Twenty-fifth Infantry Division published General Orders Number 6813, the posthumous award of the Silver Star to Captain Akos D. Szekely. It reads as follows:

> For gallantry in action: Captain Szekely distinguished himself by heroic actions on 11 September 1968, while serving as Commanding Officer with Company A, 1st Battalion, 5th Infantry near Ben Cui, Republic of Vietnam. His unit was established in its night location when they came under intense fire from a numerically superior enemy force. Captain Szekely immediately ran to the perimeter through heavy enemy fire in order to direct his men's suppressive fire on the insurgents. He continued to brave the fierce enemy shelling as he returned to his command post and directed counter mortar and artillery fire on the advancing enemy. With complete disregard for his own personal safety, he moved about the bullet swept area, and while engaging the enemy with his M-16 rifle, Captain Szekely was mortally wounded. His valorous actions contributed immeasurably to the successful completion of the mission and the defeat of the enemy force. Captain Szekely's personal bravery, aggressiveness, and devotion to duty are in keeping with the highest traditions of the military service and reflect great

credit upon himself, his unit, the 25th Infantry
Division, and the United States Army.

That Akos Szekely would risk his life for his country did
not surprise anyone who knew him, for he was the consum-
mate warrior and patriot. The fact that he, an officer in the
Corps of Engineers, sacrificed his life while commanding an
infantry company in combat did attract considerable attention. But then again, those who really knew "Zek" could easily understand that he would unselfishly do whatever possible to help his country accomplish its mission. Even though
he had already spent almost a year as an engineer company
commander in the division's Sixty-third Engineer Battalion,
he extended his tour of duty in Vietnam because of the need
for top-notch officers to command infantry companies. It was
indeed uncommon for a non-infantry officer to be selected
for such a challenging and dangerous job, but when Zek volunteered he was immediately grabbed up. It was another
amazing chapter in the amazing life of an amazing person.
Unfortunately, however, for Zek, it was his last chapter.

Life began for Zek on 24 March 1942 in Budapest, Hungary, where he was born into a military family. As one of four
fallen warriors of '64 who were only children, he was all his
parents had. Both his grandfathers were distinguished generals in the Hungarian Army and his father was a graduate of
the Hungarian Military Academy. When the Second World
War ended in Europe in 1945, Zek's father was a captain, but
the family fled to Germany because they opposed the occupation of their homeland by the Russians.

While in Germany, awaiting the opportunity to go to the
United States, one of Zek's young Hungarian playmates was
Huba Wass de Czege, who would also join West Point's Class
of '64 years later. Huba recently commented: "What a great
surprise to find out during "Beast Barracks" that Akos and I
were classmates! We hadn't seen each other since we left Germany because our families settled in different places in the

USA. We continued our good friendship as cadets and were often together even though we were in different companies. Besides being in many of the same classes, we both were on the track and cross-country teams and belonged to the Russian Club. Akos was so gifted, mentally and physically, that it made me proud to be linked with him. He also had a great disposition and boundless energy. When I heard about his death, I felt like part of me had been torn away. A valuable part of our army was lost that day for Akos had unlimited potential as an officer." (Both of our class's Hungarian Americans were outstanding cadets, officers, and leaders. Huba became one of '64's general officers. What might Akos have achieved?)

The Szekely family finally arrived in the United States in 1951 and settled in Silver Spring, Maryland, just outside the nation's capital.

Young Akos accepted the new challenge at hand. He made new friends, mastered the English language, and excelled in academics and athletics in grade school and at Montgomery Blair High School. In high school he was a member of the National Honor Society, the Mathematics Honor Society, the Key Club, and was president of the Varsity Club. Zek was the captain of the track and cross-country teams and he also played on the football, basketball, and soccer teams at one time or another. His track coach said he "had more drive and perseverance than any boy I have ever known. ... This is the most outstanding young man it has been my privilege to work with. ..."

During his senior year Zek began the process of competing for an appointment to West Point. He had been reading and hearing a lot about the academy and knew it was what he wanted—a strong education and the opportunity to serve his country. Representative John R. Foley, Sixth Maryland District, reported his selection from the large number of finalists with this remark: "Akos Szekely...the most unique, special, and outstanding student I ever appointed to the United States Military Academy."

Zek adapted well at West Point—he was a soldier by instinct. He was very proud of his ancestry, but was equally proud of his newly adopted country. By his actions and speech, he displayed his loyalty and sense of duty, as well as gratitude for the opportunities the United States and West Point afforded him. He accepted discipline as one of the necessities of life and had little tolerance for anyone who complained about limitations or who indulged in self-pity.

Zek's manner was reserved, stately, and dignified, but also intense and calculating when approaching a challenge. As a cadet he was a star performer, just as he was in high school. He ranked near the top in all of his academic courses and graduated number five in the class on 3 June 1964, and has been recognized as the highest ranking graduate of Hungarian ancestry from any of the United States Service Academies. Active and well rounded, Zek was on the Public Information Office Detail, the Debate Council and Forum, a member of the Russian Club and a letter winner on the cross-country and track teams. He also picked up the sport of long distance racewalking and took first place honors in several events, thus distinguishing himself as one of America's best. His mentor in racewalking was another of America's best, Ron Zinn, of the Class of '62 and the U.S. Olympic Team. How tragic and ironic that Ron would also die in Vietnam!

Akos spent his last two years in Company I-2, a rather raucous group that shared the "lost fifties" with M-2. Dick Nowak, our football captain and All-American, was there with him and has recalled their times together: "Akos lent a dignified side of the ledger to the otherwise vulgar brawl. As I remember, he was always smiling—a rarity for the likes of myself to recognize this particular trait. He still retained a portion of his Hungarian accent on certain words, and I, as a former Polish second-generation transplant would tease him about the Central European supremacy of the Poles.

"Wayne Richard, a roommate of mine, had had Akos as a roommate earlier and recounted an interesting side of his feelings towards the 1960's civil rights movement. Wayne was from the deep South (Alabama). Their discussions would center around Akos' belief that such a movement was needed in order to gain what he perceived as a fundamental right under the constitution. Wayne spent many hours discussing the difficulty the South had in adjusting to what they knew was a sweeping change in the land. Akos' concern centered on the inability of our citizens to relate to accepting this change. I suspect the freedoms that we take for granted and subscribe to, but sometimes implement slowly, caused him concern. This probably is understandable given his background in Hungary and the futile attempts of the Freedom Fighters in the '50s.

"Akos and I continually kidded around about track and cross-country's long-term development for the army versus football's role in preparation for our military careers. As far as long-term conditioning and individual stamina, I would concede he was correct. However, as far as teamwork and the individual within the 'wheel,' I argued that there was no substitute for the group working together. We probably were both right in our own ways, but unable at the time to accept each other's views. When it was all said and done, though, Akos certainly proved to be the ultimate team player.

"I would tease him about his racewalking. Racewalking was relatively new at the time and many times in the halls I would give a caricature impression of racewalking. This, I remember, appeared funny at the time—a lumbering lineman attempting to imitate the 'racewalker trot' in the halls of the 'lost fifties.' I suspect this provided humor for all onlookers. Although racewalking was his passion, he was an excellent distance runner in cross-country as well as a one and two miler in track.

"Perhaps what I remember most about this quite reserved but friendly classmate was his willingness to help others at any time, and his feeling of passion for the importance of freedom that the USA provided. In addition, I sensed a deep concern and 'hurt' when the talk moved to his ethnic Hungary. Our political decisions of the 1950s, which failed to aid the Hungarian Freedom Fighters, seemed still an open wound. A proud Hungarian American 'product' who had high standards, and still managed in a quiet way to be a part of I-2's style, Akos was also a great American and a great friend. His death was a shock to us all, but it typified his selflessness, patriotism, and sense of duty."

After graduation and Airborne and Ranger training, Zek was stationed in Korea for thirteen months where he eventually commanded the Fiftieth Engineer Company of the Thirteenth Engineer Battalion. In doing so, he was one of the first men in the class to command a company.

In September 1966 he entered graduate school at Massachusetts Institute of Technology in Boston and received a master of science in engineering only nine months later. During that time he also completed another special course at Harvard University and was invited to become a member of the Honorary Fraternity, Sigma Xi. While a student, he wrote, "I am aware that a good number of my friends are overseas, living in danger. Then I recall that after Massachusetts Institute of Technology my turn must surely come to live in the jungle. Over the long run, it equals out."

And, soon enough, Captain Akos Szekely left his civilian comfort. In October 1967 he arrived in Cu Chi, South Vietnam, the home of the Twenty-fifth Infantry Division. Close by, near Ben Cui, eleven months later, Zek's rapid, but overwhelmingly successful run through life would end. He was laid to rest in Arlington National Cemetery on 26 September 1968.

Only a week later, on the fourth of October, The United States Citizens of Hungarian Descent formed a committee which established an award named after Zek. The award is described in the Congressional Record dated 21 April 1969 in a speech by the Honorable Gilbert Gude, Maryland Representative, part of which is quoted:

> The representatives of the American Hungarian Federation, the Collegiate Society of Hungarian Veterans (MHBK) and the Hungarian Freedom Fighters Federation in Greater Washington and the City of Baltimore decided that, in recognition of excellence in spirit, mind and body as well as demonstrated loyalty to the United States of America, an award named AKOS SZEKELY MEMORIAL MEDAL will be established.
>
> It was also intended to perpetuate the example of Captain Szekely, who was killed in action in Vietnam, whose character traits, academic excellence and heroic death reflect the finest heritage of the Hungarian nation as well as of the Americans of Hungarian descent.
>
> The Akos Szekely Memorial Medal is awarded those United States citizens of Hungarian descent who:
>
> a. were found as deserving the award because of their excellence in spirit, mind and body, and because of their demonstrated loyalty to the United States of America.
>
> b. as citizens of the United States of America, completed their legally required or voluntarily assumed military service honorably.
>
> c. demonstrated their adherence to the values of their Hungarian heritage.
>
> d. are under 30 years of age. This age limit may be disregarded in instances when the prospective recipient was killed in action in defense of the United States of America or was highly decorated for heroism or other unusual form of military service.

The Akos Szekely Memorial Medal is awarded annually and is issued to the recipients in the month of October, possibly in close connection with the commemoration of the Hungarian struggle for freedom in 1956.

Another of Zek's great admirers in this world was army track coach, Carleton R. Crowell, who wrote his obituary, ending it with the following words: "Those of us who knew Zek will never forget him, and those who are yet to become acquainted with him will forever honor him. He had a trust in mankind and a conviction that right would triumph over wrong, not because man is destined to succeed, but because he is determined to succeed."

No nation, be it said, could have had a nobler son.

Chapter Sixteen

Carl J. Winter, Jr.

Always ready to help a buddy out of a jam, Carl is a good natured type of guy who has made many friends during his four years here at West Point. He makes his home in Hemlock, Michigan and looks forward to a career in the Engineers. However the cards may fall, Carl's amiable disposition and sense of duty point to a promising future.

Just a little over two months after Akos Szekely, a non-infantryman, was killed leading a Twenty-fifth Infantry Division infantry company in battle it happened again. Armor Captain Carl J. Winter, Jr., Zek's classmate and good friend, died while serving his country on 23 November 1968, also while leading an infantry company of the Twenty-fifth. Like Zek, Carl was a true patriot and a team player. Knowing that there were not enough qualified infantry captains to command the division's thirty-six infantry companies, he volunteered to take command of one, despite the danger of heavy enemy activity in the division's area around Cu Chi. After all, Carl had already been a successful company commander and he was Airborne and Ranger qualified—definite plusses for infantry command duty. Besides, Carl was proud to be a part of the "Tropic Lightning" Division and its honorable combat history in the Pacific Theatre. After being formed on 10 October 1941 in Hawaii, it participated in Guadalcanal and several other island campaigns in World War II, and later also took part in the Korean conflict.

The Twenty-fifth began deployment to Vietnam in late March 1966 and a few weeks later KB Kindleberger became its first '64 KIA. Its second '64 victim was David Bujalski, the following year. As it was throughout the country, 1968 was the most active year of combat for the "Tropic Lightning" Division in Vietnam as it lost Akos and Carl. Jim Kotrc (Chapter 20) would fall in 1969, also while commanding an infantry company (although he was an infantryman). On 8 December 1970 the division began deployment back to Hawaii where it has remained. Between 1993 - 1995 its commander was Major General George Fisher, USMA 1964.

128

Interestingly enough, Zek and Carl and the subsequent fallen warriors of the class died while on extended time in the army. (David Ramsay, U.S. Air Force, Chapter 23, did not fall into this category.) What happened was that when the class graduated, all those who were commissioned in the army faced a four-year commitment (a few years before it had been a three-year commitment and several years later it would go up to five years). However, before any officers could resign their commission at the four-year point, the army put out a directive adding eighteen months to the commitment (that was done because of the manpower requirements for Vietnam). It is not known who in the class may have left the army after four years, but technically speaking, service after June 1968 was considered an extension. Although the extension applied to other officer groups as well, for the Class of '64 it turned out to be another "surprise in store for '64."

Although he was born in Saginaw, Michigan, Carl was raised nearby, on a small farm in Hemlock, a tiny town of 800 people. His father, Carl, Sr., after serving in World War II as a technical sergeant in the Army Air Corps, bought the eighty-acre farm from his father, Conrad. He also worked for General Motors, and as a consequence, relied heavily on his children to help with the many farm chores. He was a lucky father, for Carl, the oldest, loved the farm and virtually ran the entire operation, including a small dairy herd, during his high school years. Carl was able to practice his leadership skills as he supervised his younger brothers, Dan and Chuck, and his sister, Mary, as they shared their numerous responsibilities beginning at dawn every day. Carl still had enough energy and strength left to earn letters on the football and golf teams and serve as the vice president and salutatorian of his 1960 graduating class at Hemlock High School.

Unlike his Iowa farmer classmate, Jim Powers, who was militarily motivated by a junior ROTC officer, Carl had never been exposed to the military nor did he have strong guidance counseling. By chance, however, the counselor had just received information from West Point shortly before talking to Carl about his college plans and suggested that he might consider applying since he met all the selection criteria. Carl's dad had always spoken highly of his military days and their small midwestern town was about as mid-American and patriotic as they come, so Carl applied, but figured his chances were slim since only about ten percent of applicants gained entrance and no one in his school district had ever even applied to any academy. Needless to say, it was a grand event in the small high school and town when Carl received notification of his acceptance.

Despite his lack of a military background, Carl adjusted quite smoothly to academy life. In fact, after rising before dawn his entire life on the farm, sleeping until 5:50 A.M. was a luxury for him. Carl was well liked by all and his cadet resume was ample. Noteworthy was his membership in the Debate Council and Forum (along with eleven other fallen warriors of the class) and his captaincy of the Bowling Club. He was also a Dean's List student and graduated in the top thirty percent of the class. Fred Pope, Carl's roommate for part of their time together in Company F-1 during firstie year, recalls the pleasure of knowing Carl and the sadness of his death: "It was hard to believe that Carl was killed in Vietnam. To those of us who knew him, he was the kind of person that should never have had anything bad happen to him—he was so good! He was tall, smart, athletic, and personable. Carl would do anything for his family and friends—and he always did it with a smile. He was extremely well rounded and fit easily into any situation whether it be an athletic contest, coaching academics, drinking beer, or going to church. His was the first loss of our cow and firstie bunch in F-1 and it really hurt. Then when Bill Black, also of F-1, died three and a half months later, it just didn't seem fair."

A month after Carl graduated and was commissioned in the armor, his brother Dan followed in his footsteps and joined the Class of 1968. Dan had always been tremendously proud of his older brother and looked upon him as a mentor and example. Through Carl's letters he learned a lot about the academy and developed a keen interest in becoming a member of the corps. During his junior year in high school Dan visited his brother at West Point, and after that, there was no doubt in his mind about where he wanted to attend college. You see, during that visit Dan lived the life of a cadet for a week—Carl and his classmates put him up in various rooms (to keep him away from the authorities) and kept him dressed in the appropriate uniform as he marched to meals and other activities. It was Carl's way of sharing his academy experience with his brother and helping to prepare him to decide on his future. The sixteen-year-old from the small farm in Michigan was completely sold. Of course, that week he lived the life of an upperclassman. As such, when he later suffered through the tough times of "Beast Barracks" and RECONDO Week, he at least was able to realize that life as a cadet would get better.

When Dan graduated in 1968, younger brother Chuck entered the Air Force Academy and later graduated with the Class of 1972. As with Dan, the main inspiration for Chuck was Carl, whom he had the opportunity to see as a cadet and as a professional officer. Carl fit the mold perfectly—tall, dark, handsome, physically fit, intelligent, and with a smile as big as Michigan.

Beverly Richards, from Bay City, Michigan, was impressed with that package when she happened to meet Carl at the swimming pool of a small golf club in Hemlock during the summer of 1963. Carl was immediately smitten and asked her out. From that point on there was no one else for Carl and they were married a year later. After Airborne and Ranger Schools, the happy young couple spent an exciting year and a half in Germany as Carl patrolled the East German border with the Second Squadron, Ninth Armored Cavalry Regiment. Despite Carl's small paycheck, the exchange rate at that time of four marks to a dollar enabled them to enjoy life somewhat.

131

The Winters returned from Germany in the summer of 1966 and were stationed at Fort Lewis, Washington, where Carl served as a company commander of a basic training company. He had had such short notice to take over that job that he and Beverly were not able to wait for their car (1964 Corvair Monza convertible) to arrive in port on the East Coast and then drive it across the country. So, Carl had Dan pick it up at the Brooklyn Navy Yard and drive it to Highland Falls where he hid it in a rented garage while he served as a squad leader in "Beast Barracks." After that, while on summer leave in August, Dan drove the car to Michigan, picked up little brother Chuck, continued the drive across the top of the country and delivered it intact to Carl and Beverly. It was a great experience for Dan and Chuck, and although the mission was accomplished, Dan wondered, "Would I have been willing to let my younger brothers do that with the new car I got when I graduated?"

Carl was recognized as a truly outstanding company commander, and he and Beverly enjoyed living in the great Northwest. The highlight of their stay there was the birth of their son, Curt. As an infant, Curt was unique in that he would only go to sleep if Carl put him in the car and drove him around the block—over and over until he dozed off. Curt has since grown up to be a fine young man. He was graduated from Michigan State University and at the time of this writing works in sales in Lansing, Michigan. His father would be extremely proud.

In late summer of 1967 Carl was designated to attend the Armor Officer Advanced Course at Fort Knox. One of his classmates there was Jeff Louis, who was also a classmate from West Point. Jeff remembers those days well: "We had a lot of classes together at the Armor School, and Patt and I lived about two blocks from Bev and Carl on the post. I hadn't known Carl well as a cadet, but at Fort Knox it didn't take long for me to realize that he was a rock-solid guy, a true family man, and an ideal representative of West Point and the Class of '64. He was a pleasure to be with, both in the classroom and socially. Curt was a baby while we were there and since Patt was pregnant with our first child we paid close attention to the way Bev and Carl took care of him. We learned a lot about loving care!

"One thing that stands out in my memory is our league bowling team. We had a great team and shared lots of laughs during the friendly competition. But fate was not on our side because not long after we all departed Fort Knox, Carl and another officer, half of our four-man team, were killed in combat.

"Patt and I were stationed at Fort Carson when we got the bad news in November. We dropped everything and made the trip to Hemlock. The whole town turned out for the funeral, despite the bitter cold. The Winter family displayed their strength and stoicism but we knew how they must have hurt inside. We all hurt.

"Patt and I have maintained contact with Beverly over the years. We're happy that she has adjusted and has a new life. For us it has been a way to keep Carl in our hearts."

After the course, Carl swore Dan in as a second lieutenant during June Week, 1968, at West Point. He then settled Beverly and Curt in Bay City, near her family, and headed for Vietnam where he initially was assigned as the S-3 Air of the Fourth Battalion, Ninth Infantry, for two months. Carl then had a choice of being a general's aide or an infantry company commander. He opted for the more risky challenge of commanding a company in combat. Company C had had the reputation of being the worst company in the battalion, but Carl quickly got it in shape and the unit participated in several successful combat operations. Misfortune struck, however, on 23 November, when, after an airmobile assault, C Company was pinned down in an open, dry rice paddy by a larger enemy force in an adjacent wooded area. The fighting was fierce and Carl and his men held the enemy off long enough until a friendly unit was able to reinforce C Company and together they overcame the Viet Cong. C Company suffered several casualties, though, because of a lack of protection in the rice paddy. Most significant among them was the commander, Captain Carl Winter, who was killed instantly by a hail of bullets. It was a tough way to earn the Bronze Star with "V" and the Purple Heart. Carl had already been awarded several other medals to include the Combat Infantryman's Badge.

Carl's death was a great shock to his small hometown and especially to his parents. As the oldest son, he was their hero and their strength. Their lives were never the same again. They sold the farm and now live in an apartment in Saginaw. Beverly and Carl's brothers and sister have had to go on. Beverly eventually remarried and she raised Curt to be a model citizen.

Years after Carl's death, Dan, in writing his brother's obituary, expressed concern that he would not be able to do justice to someone so special: "...an older brother who you knew cared about you and would always be there when you needed him." Dan summed it up as follows: "Carl's life is best described by one word: Love. He had a deep and abiding love of life, love of family, and love of God and Country. It permeated every aspect of his life, and everyone who had the privilege of knowing him was touched by it in some way. I have often asked myself how a person with so much to give could be taken from us so early. The answer to that question has eluded me for many years. As the years have passed the answer has slowly emerged—he has never really left us. Yes, he is gone from us physically, but he has left an indelible watermark by which we can measure the successes and failures of our lives. Carl was sent to us for a very special purpose and left us having completely and wonderfully accomplished it. ... We feel your presence constantly among us and realize that for all things there is a purpose. For twenty-five years the earth was a better place because you were here, and it will be a better place for many years to come because of what you left behind. The memories of our times together are treasures which can never be lost.

"Farewell, my dear brother, until we meet again."

Chapter Seventeen

William Ray Black

Bill came to West Point with a "no sweat" attitude and left
with it. This good natured likeable guy, who had no worries
for four years, spent a majority of his time staying as far away
from the T.D. and Academic Departments as possible. Bill's
ability and personality insure success in the future.

D uring the summer of 1963, Cadet William Ray Black
was assigned as the first sergeant of the Second New
Cadet Company. His mission, along with the rest of
the cadre of first and second classmen, was to prepare the new
cadets of the Class of 1967 for acceptance into the Corps of
Cadets. At that time, Major General William C. Westmoreland,
the academy's superintendent, was spending his last days on
the job before taking over as the commander of XVIII Airborne
Corps at Fort Bragg. (Several months later he was assigned
as the deputy commander of USMACV and then became the
commander in June 1964.) The Class of 1964 and General
Westmoreland had been together for the previous three years
and had developed a considerable amount of mutual respect.
But then the "Westy Incident" occurred—it was an event
which added a rich chapter to the lore and history of the class.

At about five o'clock in the afternoon of the day before
the general's departure, a beautiful day filled with sunshine
and blue skies, Westy (as he was affectionately referred to)
was returning from the library tennis courts on his way home
to the Supe's quarters when he jogged by several stalwart
members of the Class of '64 who were resting and sunning
themselves on a set of parade field bleachers that aligned the
plain (Bill Black was not in that illustrious group.). As luck
would have it, our classmates failed to see General
Westmoreland's approach and did not jump to attention or
render a salute and proper military courtesies. Westy took
exception to this state of affairs and promptly "chewed out"
our somewhat dazed and contrite classmates. In a moment,
the Supe departed...our classmates resumed the "rest and sun"
position...and the incident was ended.

Or so it was thought!

That night, the "King of Beasts," the New Cadet Barracks Battalion Commander, Dick Chilcoat, received word from the Cadet Officer of the Guard to assemble all first-class members of the cadre (several hundred strong) in Central Area after reveille. Assembly was at the direction of the superintendent no less.

Dick was more than happy to perform the task. It was to be General Westmoreland's last day at West Point, and he obviously wanted to extol the virtues of the Class of '64. After all, we had been "Westy's Class" because we had been in residence at USMA during his entire tenure as superintendent.

The next morning, with Bill and his classmates standing smartly at attention in formation, Dick Chilcoat reported to the Supe as he mounted the stoops in Central Area, "Sir, the Class of 1964 is all present and accounted for!" The commandant, BG Michael S. Davison, was standing to the rear of the Supe observing intently.

Then, after receiving the report, to the amazement of all present, General Westmoreland proceeded to administer a ten-minute tongue-lashing to the class about the implications of failing to salute senior officers and a lesson in military courtesy and traditions. Throughout, all the firsties present stood at attention, in shock, and in dismay.

At the end of the stern lecture, General Westmoreland saluted, ordered Chilcoat to "take charge," wheeled away, returned to his quarters, and several hours later departed West Point for his new assignment—all in all, an extraordinary departure from West Point. BG Davison called Chilcoat forward and asked, "What was that all about?" Dick lamely replied, "I have no idea, sir; I'll find out."

It wasn't long until the entire story unfolded about what had happened (or failed to happen) on the plain the day prior. It was clear that General Westmoreland, the soldier's soldier, decided to "leave a mark" on the Class of '64 and capitalized on the event to "mentor" the class at large. His unusual departure "ceremony" was not just about military courtesy and traditions—it was about the fundamental truths of West Point and its motto: Duty, Honor, Country. He was building "leaders of character" even then.

The "Westy Incident" concluded, after much mentoring and coaching by BG Davison, with a Class of 1964 letter of apology to General Westmoreland signed by Dick Chilcoat, who was also the class president, in which fault was acknowledged and forgiveness was sought. Indeed, no offense was ever intended.

In several weeks, Westy responded in a short, but gracious letter saying all was forgiven and forgotten.

Forgotten? For General Westmoreland—yes. For the Class of '64—the "Westy Incident" endures forever! For Bill Black it was another important lesson learned as he finished the summer without further incident and returned to Company F-1 for his final year at West Point.

Bill was born in Newbern, Tennessee, on 19 April 1942, the son of Marjorie T. Black and O. L. Black. Brother James joined the family four years later. Bill grew up nearby in Dyer and attended Dyer High School where he established a solid record of achievement and graduated as the class valedictorian in 1960. Besides belonging to the Cumberland Presbyterian Youth Fellowship, he had been president of his class and the Beta Club and an Eagle Scout.

Bill secured a congressional appointment from the Eighth Congressional District of Tennessee and entered West Point a month later. For not having had a military background, Bill performed exceptionally well in "Beast Barracks." His strong character traits of discipline, devotion to duty, hard work, self-effacement, and good humor served him well. He was cool and confident under pressure and always remained good-natured and likeable.

Academics presented more of a challenge to Bill than the military and physical requirements. Consequently, he worked hard at the arduous task of mastering the cadet curriculum. Plebe math was especially challenging, but Bill won out, and as his grasp of the situation grew firmer, he was able to devote more time to numerous extracurricular activities such as the Astronomy Club, Debate Council and Forum, French Club, Rocket Society, Bowling Club, Outdoor Sportsman Club, Scoutmasters Council, Ski Club, Pointer Magazine Staff, and the Protestant Cadet Fellowship Group. To say he was well rounded would be an understatement.

Bill was not enamored of the weather at West Point. He often would quote from Robert Service's famous poem about Sam McGee from Tennessee. Bill was never warm during the New York winters. He lamented often about the hospitable climate of his native state and rued the day he moved north of the Mason-Dixon line. It was especially cold during "Plebe Christmas" in 1960 as the Class of '64 was one of the last classes that had to remain at the academy during the holiday season of their plebe year.

Bill's greatest achievement was his successful courtship of the lovely Anne Shirley Deubler whom he had met at one of the Saturday night hops at Camp Buckner during the summer of 1961. They were wed on 31 July 1965.

Branch selection was easy for Bill. Only one branch ever held his interest, and upon graduation he was commissioned in his beloved infantry. Being the dedicated, adventurous outdoorsman that he was, he breezed through the Airborne and Ranger courses. Former roommate, Pat Graves, recalls an incident in Ranger School: "During the Florida phase (There were three phases—one at Fort Benning, one in the mountains of Dahlonega, Georgia, and one in the swamps of Florida at Eglin Air Force Base. Later, a desert phase was added at Dugway Proving Grounds, Utah, which even later was changed to Fort Bliss, Texas.) the class was formed in a large circle, receiving instruction. Suddenly, a large rattlesnake slithered into the ring. Any thought that the cadre had staged the event was quickly dispelled when the instructor fled. Everyone scattered except Bill, who calmly picked up a stick, pinned the reptile's head to the ground, and then picked it up. We all had known that he would make a great infantry-man and that act confirmed it."

Bill's initial army assignment was with the Second Battalion, 501st Airborne Infantry Regiment, 101st Airborne Division at Fort Campbell, Kentucky. He was not there for long, though, for the build-up of U.S. Forces in Vietnam was causing the curtailment of most assignments in the States and Europe. As a result, Bill was sent to be an advisor to the Sixth Battalion of the South Vietnamese Airborne Brigade in March 1966. Three months later Anne gave birth to their son, William Geoffrey. (The middle name was for their good friend, classmate Geoffrey Kleb—in fact, the youngster would always be called "Geof.")

After a safe and successful tour in Vietnam, during which time he was promoted to captain, Bill returned home in April 1967 and was assigned to the Ranger Department of the U.S. Army Infantry School at Fort Benning. Those were very busy times, as the Ranger Department had the important mission of preparing young officers for combat in Vietnam. Bill's experience was put to good use and his outstanding performance led to his being selected as aide-de-camp to Major General John M. Wright, Jr., Commanding General, U.S. Army Infantry Center and Fort Benning, and Commandant, U.S. Army Infantry School. The Blacks were comfortable and happy at Fort Benning. Bill was enjoying his challenging job and Anne was enjoying teaching school. They both shared the enjoyment of raising young Geof.

In Southeast Asia the war was raging on and the U.S. troop strength maintained its peak level of just over 540,000 from early 1968 through mid-1969. Many officers, especially those in the infantry, had already had two tours in Vietnam. The turn-around time for infantry captains at that time was eighteen to twenty-four months.

Accordingly, after twenty-two months in the States, infantry captain Bill Black had to leave his family at Fort Benning early in 1969 and return to the combat zone where he joined the Second Battalion, Twelfth Cavalry of the First Cavalry Division. After a few short weeks as the S-2, he assumed command of Company A, and, while leading that unit against a superior force, was killed in action on 8 March 1969, just three weeks after his arrival back in Vietnam. Bill was the Class of '64's first victim of 1969.

Bill's long list of awards, headed by a Silver Star and three Bronze Stars (with "V"), was impressive but was small consolation for his family, his classmates, and his soldiers. He had been a down-to-earth, easygoing friend to all. His former roommate, Richard Carr, later recalled: "Billy Ray, as he was known to his friends, was one of those people who dealt with just what life presented to him. He was a great roommate; easy to talk with, always willing to take time to listen, one who could laugh at himself or ludicrous situations in a way that relaxed any who were in his presence. Bill was a giver and not a taker; not a particularly competitive person—which, when you think about it, probably contributed to his really relaxed attitude amongst so many well-developed egos. He was interested in his friends, especially the love of his life, Anne, whom he saw at every opportunity.

"Billy Ray had a deep, resonating voice with a laugh that seemed to shake his whole body. He had a 'street sense' about him that served him well and a basic intelligence that kept him on the straight and narrow. He could be heard engaging in lively discussion on politics, life, or perhaps the deeper meaning of the latest 'flick' he had seen.

"He was the type of person that you just know would have been a great husband, father, and contributor to his community. It is tragic that this 'salt of the earth' human being could be taken from his loved ones at such an early age. He enjoyed the immense private pleasures of Anne and Geof."

At the time of this writing Anne continues to teach school at Fort Benning and Geof has graduated from college with a marketing degree and is employed in that field in Columbus, Georgia.

One of the last classmates to see Bill alive was Jed Brown, who was on a short break at the Vung Tau R&R site in early March. Bill was also there for a day before taking over his infantry company, the only day off he was supposed to have for the rest of his tour. The two had been company-mates in F-1 during their last two cadet years. Among the million things they chatted about was the recent death of their F-1 buddy, Carl Winter. They also lamented the loss of several other classmates, including Kirby Wilcox and Mike Nawrosky, who had also been in the First Cav the year before. As they sipped their beer there was no way to know that Bill would become the class's seventeenth fallen warrior only a few days later. And, how sad for Jed again a little over a year later when Alex Hottell (Chapter 22) perished a day after relaxing over a beer with Jed and Jim Carson in the First Cav's Officers Club tent.

They say, "the good die young." Bill was twenty-six years of age when he died, which was the average age of the twenty-four victims of the Class of '64 when they died. His devotion to West Point and the precepts of "Duty, Honor, Country," to which must be added "Family," framed his life. Bill left behind a personal touch and many fond memories that still warm those who knew and loved him. His every action reflected great credit on himself, his family, his alma mater and his country.

Spring was just around the corner when Bill Black was laid to rest in the West Point Cemetery.

Chapter Eighteen

Gerard Vincent Palma

Few of us will ever forget the ready smile and easy going disposition of this South Jerseyite, Jerry Palma. Jerry was always ready to help out a classmate or give him a home on a weekend, in spite of the fact that the T.D. may have kept him "boning character" back at West Point. An armor file from Camp Buckner days, he will certainly be an asset to his branch of the service.

Gerry Palma became the eighteenth warrior of the Class of '64 to fall in combat when he died a soldier's death on 19 April 1969. And, just as were several of the other casualties in the class, Gerry was on his second voluntary tour of duty in the combat zone.

Gerard Vincent Palma grew up in Hammonton, New Jersey, the son of Agatha and Joseph Palma and the younger brother of Ann. Theirs was a close, loving family, and Gerry was raised under the highest of ethical standards. Throughout his childhood and youth, he was committed to a life of service to his fellow man. After graduating from Hammonton High School in 1959 he entered Georgetown University in Washington, D.C., where he pondered his next step in life. His dilemma was that he was desirous of serving mankind as either a priest or a soldier—both professions appealed to him. One day in the spring of 1960, while he was in the Georgetown Chapel seeking divine guidance, his acceptance to West Point arrived in the form of a principal appointment from the Second Congressional District of New Jersey. That decided the issue and Gerry entered the academy with the intensity, drive, and commitment that were to characterize his all-too-short life. On the athletic field, in the classroom, or at home providing hospitality for classmates who lived too far away for their parents to visit, Gerry set demanding personal standards.

One of those classmates who enjoyed the hospitality of the Palma home was fellow Italo-American, Dave Baratto, from Mount Shasta, California. Dave recounts the following effort to reciprocate during the summer of 1963 after AOT in Germany: "I had planned to take my one-month leave in Europe with the intent of visiting my relatives (whom I had never

145

met before) somewhere in Northern Italy. Somewhat reluctant to venture out on my own, I thought I would ask Gerry if he might like to accompany me. Without hesitation, Gerry was quick and warm with his response. 'Sure, Dave, if you really want me to go.'

"We took the train to Bassano; from there I called my relatives to come pick us up. Cousin Domenico arrived a couple of hours later on a Vespa motor scooter and began to shuttle us and our two bags to Possagno—a process that took about half a day. Gerry couldn't speak any Italian, but by the time we left there he was part of the family. We climbed Mount Grappa, put on Twist Dance Demo's, and harvested the crops in the field. To this day, every time I see my relatives, they recall the fond memories they have of their friend, Gerry Palma. Recently, when they visited us in Washington, D.C., they indicated that one of the places they wanted to see was the Vietnam Memorial. We visited it and quietly searched for our friend's etched name on the wall. The only comment upon finding the name was, 'CHE PECCA' (What a shame)." (Major General David Baratto had the opportunity to see a lot of his relatives in Northern Italy when he was assigned there from 1992 - 1994 as the Southern European Task Force Commander.)

Another classmate who became close to Gerry and his family was Cris Stone, who relates the following: "Gerry and I were roommates for two years. When cadet companies were reshuffled, we became roommates by accident in I-1. With his New Jersey Yankee accent and my southern West Virginia hillbilly twang, we wondered if we would ever be able to understand each other. By first-class year, we had invested so much time in learning to understand the other's strange language that we continued to room together. We were good friends, too."

Twenty years after his death, Gerry's sister, Ann, received a letter from his classmate Marty Michlik, which said: "I first met Gerry in my Beast Company. I remember running next to

146

him on the way to Target Field. We were both from New Jersey and we got together frequently. We both went Armor. We went through Airborne School together and were Ranger buddies...he loved the stress and physical demands of both Airborne and Ranger. He threw himself into the training. I don't think Gerry was capable of doing anything halfway. I don't think he ever in his life pulled a punch or tried to take a shortcut."

Upon graduation from West Point, Gerry celebrated with the only personal indulgence many of us remember—a Corvette—his graduation present to himself. The Corvette was an extremely popular car among the bachelors in the class. Its price tag in 1964 was around $3,600. Some of the men in the class who got married had also purchased Corvettes but ended up selling them within a few months. It seems that there wasn't enough trunk space for their wives' suitcases. But Gerry was happy with his and after Airborne and Ranger Schools he hopped in it to drive to Fort Carson, Colorado, for his initial assignment. Marty Michlik remembers that trip: "Both of us were assigned to Fort Carson, and we arranged to drive out in tandem. In the middle of a January night I had car problems and fell out. Gerry went on. After some time he realized I was not still behind him and doubled back to find and help me. I remember the two of us, sitting on a dark highway in Kansas, unhappy with our state of affairs, but confident that we would work any problem out, though it might take a number of hours. I was happy I had Gerry to depend on.

"After we got to Fort Carson, Gerry and I lived in the same BOQ. Both of us were assigned as recon platoon leaders. Gerry threw himself into that job with the same vigor with which he approached everything else in his life. He worked hard and did well. Gerry enjoyed being a platoon leader and liked our life in Colorado, but he was driven to do more. As a true professional, he instinctively marched to the sound of the guns and volunteered to go to Vietnam and was

147

delighted when he got assigned to the 101st. I remember he got a sponsor letter from our classmate Seth Hudgins, who was then in the 101st. I think Gerry must have read Seth's letter to me a dozen times, excited about his upcoming assignment."

He served for a year as a cavalry platoon leader in the Second Squadron, Seventeenth Cavalry. His commander there said that Gerry was "a fearless combat leader who strove for excellence in all he did. He was totally dedicated to his mission and the welfare of his men. He refused to report several minor wounds because he did not wish to be taken from his soldiers in the field."

One of his several citations for valor stated: "Serving as a platoon leader in A Troop, 2d Squadron, 17th Cavalry of the 101st Airborne Division near Tuy Hoa last March 13th, 1st Lieutenant Palma was leading a relief force to aid the badly outnumbered patrol in combat with the Vietcong. They crossed an open area under intense fire to establish a linkup, then directed artillery fire and an air strike, forcing the enemy to withdraw."

Gerry successfully completed his year in Vietnam and returned to the States where he became aide-de-camp to the commanding general, Military District of Washington. He asked to get out of that job early in order to return to Vietnam as soon as possible. Without pretense or false modesty, he said simply that there was a war going on and he was a West Point-trained soldier. In his mind nothing else needed to be said.

Before returning to Southeast Asia, he attended the Infantry Officer Advanced Course as an armor exchange officer. Cris Stone's mother cherishes the following memory of Gerry's trip to Fort Benning: "When my son was in Vietnam, I received a call from Gerry early one weekday morning. He was driving to Fort Benning and had seen a road sign and mileage marker to our small town 'only 55 miles' away. He had never visited our home, but he had roomed with my son. Gerry called and said he would like to stop by. Over the breakfast I hastily prepared, we talked and laughed, and he filled the gaps only a classmate and fellow soldier could understand. That hour-and-a-half breakfast gave my spirit a lift which endured for weeks. Two years later, when I heard of his death in combat, I cancelled everything in order to go to Arlington for the funeral so I could say to Gerry's parents how his thoughtfulness and sensitivity were a comfort to me."

After completing the Advanced Course, Gerry visited his family before returning to Vietnam. His sister, Ann, remembers his last night at home: "The night before he left for his second tour in Vietnam, he sat on the floor, leaning against the sofa with his legs stretched out and crossed. He had on a black golf shirt and khaki slacks. He talked about peace, about the Vietnamese people and their history and politics until four in the morning. He never talked about the war. That was the last time I talked with my brother."

Upon returning to Vietnam, Gerry was given the job he wanted—cavalry troop commander in the Third Squadron, Eleventh Armored Cavalry Regiment. He gave it his all, but on 19 April 1969, while leading his troop in combat from his command helicopter, he was mortally wounded. After he was wounded, his last conscious moments were spent directing retaliatory fire on those who endangered his unit. The pilot flew desperately to get Gerry to safety, but Gerry succumbed before the helicopter landed. Although he had already been decorated for valor several times, he would not be able to refuse this final Purple Heart.

Several years after his death, Gerry's family found the following lines in his handwritten personal notebook: "There are games that you play to play; there are games that you play to win; there are games that you do not play. The closest analogy I can offer people as to what I mean when I say 'I am a soldier' is that it is analogous to what I mean when I say 'I am a Catholic.' I wish to live a soldier's life, do a soldier's work, render a soldier's service, and die a soldier's death."

Gerry's death deeply affected his family and his many friends. Nine years later, upon the death of his father, Gerry's mother wrote to Cris Stone: "The spark of living had left him when Gerard was killed. My one consolation is in thinking they are together now. None of it is easy to take, but the memories are beautiful." (Agatha joined Gerry and Joe two years later.)

Cris' wife, Annette, recalls a lighter side of Gerry: "Oh Gerry! I will never forget him. He would show up at 5:45 in the evening, knowing he was always welcome at our dinner table. Or, he would call at three in the afternoon and say, 'There is a special girl coming into town and I need a place for her to stay. I know you have a guest room.'

" 'Of course, Gerry—we would be glad to host her. When does she arrive?' (Thinking he must mean the weekend after next.)

" 'I'm at the airport right now. I will bring her by your house in forty-five minutes.' "

Dave Baratto remembers Gerry's friendship: "Gerry wasn't a super jock, a hive, a goat, or a fileboner (overly zealous student)...he was someone anybody could have as a true friend...and that's exactly what he was—a friend to everyone. Not flashy, not loud, but genuine and sincere, that was Gerry Palma to the bone. His deep respect for, and his pride in his Italo-American family, combined with his Catholic upbringing to create the ideal soldier value set. Respect, loyalty and a warm smile were givens with Gerry—and they were always present. I can't ever recall him having an agenda of his own, in fact. He was always willing to go along and fill in whenever needed. I distinctly and fondly remember that Gerry traveled across the entire country to participate in my wedding in June of 1964. Ruth and I were, and still are, awestruck by that—but that's the way Gerry was."

In his hometown of Hammonton there is a park named for and dedicated to Gerry. The money was raised by friends, teachers, coaches, and townspeople. At the U.S. Army Armor

Center in Fort Knox, Kentucky, not far from Serio Hall, there is an Armored Training Brigade building dedicated to Captain Gerard Palma because of the efforts of a classmate.

If there is a special place in the Long Gray Line for those who "find a soldier's resting place beneath a soldier's blow," then there is a special reverence when those of us who have recalled the memories of Gerry Palma say reverently, "Well Done—Be Thou At Peace."

Gerry is buried at Arlington in good company with our nation's other heroes.

Chapter Nineteen

Martin Levering Green, Jr.

From the hallowed halls of Sewanee came a Southern gentleman, a quiet, soft-spoken individual who remained undaunted
by the traditional forces of Cadet life. A man of principles, he
remained cool to those influences contrary to his purpose, yet
he dedicated himself with tenacious devotion to those things
he found to his liking. His strength of principle and individu-
alism insure respect in all those who have been and will be
fortunate enough to know him.

152

On 11 May 1969, less than a month after Gerry Palma's death, Captain Martin Green made the supreme sacrifice, that of giving his life for his country, outside Camp Ben Het, South Vietnam. Martin was an inspirational and unselfish leader and it was in an act of altruism that he lost his life on the battlefield in the defense of freedom. The citation accompanying the Silver Star Medal posthumously awarded to Martin reads in part:

> Captain Green distinguished himself by exceptionally valorous actions on 11 May 1969 while serving as the battalion commander of a mobile strike force on a search and clear mission deep within hostile territory near the Ben Het Special Forces Camp in the Central Highlands. As he was leading an element in assaulting a hill held by a large enemy force, he received a call for help from one of his platoon leaders who had been wounded by machine-gun fire and pinned down. Captain Green single-handedly fought his way across the perilous terrain through the hostile fusillade, to his wounded comrade. With complete disregard for his safety he attempted to move the casualty to a safe position. While performing this endeavor, he was mortally wounded by enemy fire.

Martin was the third member of the Class of '64 to be killed during only a little more than the first third of 1969. At such a rate, it appeared that 1969 would be a worse year for the class than 1967 and 1968, each of which claimed five of its members. U.S. troop strength in Vietnam had been over 500,000 since late 1967 and had been maintaining its peak of 543,000 from early 1968 through May 1969. Recently installed President Richard Nixon would not be able to begin his troop reduction process until the following month, June. By the end of 1969 the figure would be down to 479,000. The Class of '64, fortunately, would not maintain the high casualty rate it had through early May. The class's fourth and last fallen warrior during 1969 would be Jim Kotrc (Chapter 20) in late July. Another eleven months would pass before the death of Bob Walters (Chapter 21). Martin, Jim, and Bob were the only three victims of '64 who served with the Special Forces in Vietnam. How ironic that they died in succession!

Martin Levering Green, Jr., was born in Gorgas Hospital, in what was formerly known as the Panama Canal Zone, on 9 July 1941. His father, Colonel Martin Levering Green, Sr., a 1937 USMA graduate, was stationed there at the time. His mother, Catherine Fox Green, a graduate of George Washington University, was from Fairfax County, Virginia. (Fox Mill Road, a key artery in Fairfax County, was named after her ancestors.) Martin's brother and sister, Maurice and Jeanette, would join the family later. Martin was the first of two sons of West Point graduates in the class to die in Vietnam. The other one was Bob Walters. The two of them also graduated from Northern Virginia high schools in 1959.

Through his formative years Martin attended schools in several states and overseas. Jim Carson remembers Martin from their time together in Japan when their fathers were part of MacArthur's occupation force: "It was 1950 - 1951, back when Japan was just beginning to get its feet back on the ground after World War II. 'Butch,' as we called him then, was in the fourth grade and I was in the third. As young as we were, we really got around! We used to take a train, by ourselves, from one end of Tokyo to the other to go to the Ernie Pyle Theater for the Saturday matinees. Then we would go to the library, Officers Club and pool, etc., before hopping back on the train. Things are quite different now in Japan. Anyway, nine years later as I was boarding the bus at the Port Authority in New York City on my way to join the Class of '64, lo and behold, there was Martin, on the same bus. What a pleasant surprise! We did a rapid job of covering nine years on that short bus ride. At the academy we remained good friends, although we were never in the same company. We did walk quite a few hours together on the area as we both were members of the Century Club. Along with my roommate, Denis Galloway, the other fallen warriors of our class who were members of that esteemed organization were David Ugland and Johnny Graham (Chapter 24). I loved them all!" [Barry McCaffrey, 64's only four-star general and recently appointed National Drug Policy Director was also a proud member of the Century Club. It has to be an important organization, for many other great leaders were members, including Dwight D. Eisenhower, USMA '15.]

Martin distinguished himself in many areas during his grade school and high school years. He performed as an acolyte in the Episcopal Church, starred in the classroom and in athletics, and, as an Eagle Scout, was inducted into the Order of the Arrow and earned the God and Country Award. As a Boy Scout he earned his merit badges under the watchful eyes of army NCO's who taught him "the ropes" the same way pre-World War II NCO's had taught his father and other "shavetails" (second lieutenants). (NCO's are known as the "backbone of the army"—Cliff McKittrick (Chapter 8) provided additional evidence.) For the Eagle Scout Badge, the NCO evaluator made Martin and his own son, each separately, catch, kill, skin, cook, and eat a snake.

Martin also received the Kiwanis Inspirational Award and while attending Herndon High School in Herndon, Virginia, he served as vice president of the student council and played two years of varsity football. His reputation as a fierce but fair competitor on the gridiron attracted a scholarship offer from Western Maryland College, which he turned down be-

cause his mind was already made up to attend West Point and
become an army officer.

Being a military "brat," Martin was eligible to apply for a
presidential appointment to the academy, which he did. He
placed twenty-eighth out of over a thousand applicants, but
there was only room for twenty-six presidential appointees
in 1959 (Bob Walters also missed the cut). So, Martin attended
the University of the South in Sewanee, Tennessee, that year
and tried again. Once again, he ended up number twenty-
eight, but in 1960 there were thirty vacancies for presidential
appointees, so Martin joined the Class of '64 that summer—
along with Bob Walters.

> I, Martin L. Green, do solemnly swear that I will
> support the Constitution of the United States,
> and bear true allegiance to the National Gov-
> ernment; that I will maintain and defend the
> sovereignty of the United States paramount to
> any and all allegiance, sovereignty, or fealty I
> may owe to any State, county, or country what-
> soever; and that I will at all times obey the le-
> gal orders of my superior officers, and the rules
> and articles governing the Armies of the United
> States.

When Martin took that oath, standing tall with his new
classmates on the first day of "Beast Barracks," he realized
fully from that point on his main purpose in life was to serve
his country. As a cadet he was well known as a man of his
word, loyal and courageous, whose goal in life was to personify the Cadet Prayer, which he accepted in theory and in
fact. "...Strengthen and increase our admiration for honest
dealing and clean thinking, and suffer not our hatred of hy-
pocrisy and pretence ever to diminish. ... Endow us with the
courage that is born of loyalty to all that is noble and worthy,

that scorns to compromise with vice and injustice and knows no fear when truth and right are in jeopardy. ..."

Martin was a pillar of strength in the class and a top-notch athlete in the intramural leagues. He was also an ardent member of the Debate Council and Forum and the Parachute Club, like so many of the other fallen warriors in the class. And, like the majority of those patriots, he selected the infantry as his branch (fourteen of the twenty-four did so).

Berlin, Germany, was Martin's first assignment. His unit, the Fourth Battalion, Eighteenth Infantry, did some infantry training, but, as part of the Berlin Brigade, it was mainly a spit and polish organization. At times the unit performed guard duty at the Berlin Prison, where Rudolph Hess was kept. Since Berlin was occupied by the armies of four nations, Martin, the exemplary ambassador, mixed well with the Berliners and came to know British, French, and Russian officers who performed similar duties.

In early 1967 Martin passed through the States to attend the Infantry Officer Advanced Course and the Special Forces Orientation Course on his way to Vietnam and the Fifth Special Forces Group.

The U.S. Army Special Forces were assuming an ever-increasing role during the decade of the sixties. All but eliminated during the fifties, these elite troops began to expand in the early sixties, largely due to President John F. Kennedy's interest in them. His fascination was such that he once invited a unit of the "Green Berets" to the family home in Hyannisport, Massachusetts, to exhibit their skills. Their skills were many, as they were experts in training, jungle fighting, parachuting, civic action, and guerrilla warfare. Special Forces soldiers also have the capability of communicating anywhere in the world—in Vietnam many of them learned not only Vietnamese, but also the various dialects of the Montagnards and other indigenous elements. By the fall of 1965 there were some sixty Special Forces camps throughout Vietnam, usually located in enemy dominated territory. The 2,500 "Green Berets"

157

commanded or advised more than 60,000 Vietnamese and ethnic minorities. In addition to gathering timely and accurate intelligence in their areas, they recruited and trained local citizens as antiguerrilla soldiers and organized them as Mobile Strike Forces, the CIDG (Civilian Irregular Defense Group) Program and some Regional and Popular Force units. Most Vietnam vets would agree that our "Green Berets" exerted an impact on the war disproportionate to their numbers.

When Martin arrived in late 1967, the Special Forces efforts were establishing a standing Montagnard Army and building heavily fortified operational bases. Assigned to the Ben Het Special Forces Camp in the Central Highlands, Martin developed a deep interest in the culture of the Montagnards and their worthiness to be taught how to make their way in a democratic society. He learned to speak their dialect fluently and exhibited selfless devotion to duty by extending his tour of duty twice as he rose to be a Mobile Strike Force battalion commander. His unit consisted of another U.S. Army captain as second in command, a Special Forces medic, five Australian warrant officers as company commanders and 500 Montagnards.

When Martin made his final trip to the States for R&R, an NCO at the San Francisco airport recommended that he change into civilian clothes before leaving the airport so that the people outside wouldn't spit on him. The only problem was that Martin didn't have any civvies with him, and sure enough, he was spat upon outside the airport. When he arrived home in Virginia, his father asked why he was going back for a third tour. He replied that he and other officers had learned how to stay alive and would stay to teach others the same system. He also believed that his battalion could succeed where others had failed.

On numerous occasions Martin's battalion did succeed where others had failed. Under his inspirational leadership the unit was molded into a skilled, courageous, and tough fighting team. The profound change in the battalion's combat proficiency was regarded as remarkable by all those in a position to make a comparison. As a token of the high esteem the Montagnards held for Martin during their long and dedicated association, they awarded him a record eighteen bracelets.

When Martin returned from R&R in May 1969 his executive officer, Captain David M. Zeckser, departed on his R&R. Almost immediately Camp Ben Het came under siege by a numerically superior enemy force and they were ordered to break out and capture some reputed Chinese and North Vietnamese generals. They did so, but were ambushed by an estimated two North Vietnamese regiments. One of the warrant officers was wounded and Martin went to help him. Both were killed by machine-gun and rifle fire. The American medic was able to verify that both were dead and secured their dog tags and Martin's ring and watch. Many Montagnards were killed in the intense action and the unit was forced to retreat without being able to retrieve Martin's body. The warrant officer who bravely led the battalion's fight back to the base camp was awarded the Victoria Cross for his action. Martin's Silver Star and Purple Heart were added to his numerous previously earned awards.

By the time David Zeckser returned from Chicago and was able to direct the recovery of the body, over a month had passed. Martin Levering Green, Jr., was finally laid to rest in July in the West Point Cemetery among many of his classmates and friends.

Martin was a man of unshakable principles, who knew where he was going and could persuade others to go with him. He was extremely inspirational with his men and paid particular attention to the human element. He was convinced that the best could only be achieved through reason and right, coupled with perseverance and determination. His approach was always fresh, straightforward, and discerning, and he possessed the ability and determination to tackle many tasks that had long been in need of attention. These personal qualities were a legacy from his parents to whom he was sincerely devoted. His death was a tragic loss to them, his brother and sister, his friends around the world, the Class of '64 and the U.S. Army.

Captain David Zeckser, who knew and appreciated Martin as well as anyone, said in his obituary: "Fortunately, the impressions Martin made on those who came in contact with him over the years are indelible. His strict adherence to principles and his occasional tendency to tilt at windmills may serve as food for thought for all of us. Martin could and did differentiate between sincerity and pretence, fact and fiction, and dreams and reality. He taught his associates that although the truth may be painful, it must be endured. He professed that nothing should be hidden or whitewashed for the sake of institutional rigidities.

"I have never met a more professional soldier or dedicated officer. He loved the service and his country more than himself, but he was quick to recognize weak points in the military system and worked tenaciously toward improvement in those areas. A lesser man would have exhibited the more common passive attitude to preclude personal inconvenience.

"Surely the rest of us owe him an immeasurable debt in defense of freedom."

Chapter Twenty

James Carl Kotrc

Coming from the great state of Nebraska, Jim is well known for his avid interest in mountaineering, exceptional talent as an artist and unusual ability in getting along with members of the fairer sex. He is even better known for his never ending, but successful battle with the Academic Department and will do well in the Army as one of the more devoted members of our class.

The summer of 1964 found the Class of '64's new graduates scattered around the world, enjoying their sixty-day leave, knowing that soon it would be back to the grindstone. Some worked, most played. Some honeymooned, others partied. Jack Grubbs' in-laws, Sylvia and Bob Schultz, decided to take a trip to the Virgin Islands after Judy and Jack's wedding. One afternoon, while sitting in a cafe in St. Thomas, they observed a handsome young man stroll by and commented to each other that he appeared too military to be a typical tourist. In fact, with his perfect posture, chiseled physique, and short, neat haircut, he looked as if he had come straight from West Point. Their curiosity aroused, they hailed the gentleman and asked where he was from. By that time Sylvia and Bob were not all that surprised when the young officer replied that he had just graduated from West Point, his name was Jim Kotrc, and yes, of course, he knew his classmate Jack Grubbs. Jim was already serving as a model West Point product and would continue to do so during his brief but superlative military career.

Three and a half years earlier, on a frigid January day in the nation's capital, Jim Kotrc and the rest of the Corps of Cadets marched in President John F. Kennedy's inaugural parade. As he marched by the platform and stole a glance, Jim, like all the other parade participants, couldn't help but be impressed by the youth and vigor of the new commander in chief. The inaugural address given that day by President Kennedy was full of promises, but the words which probably resounded around the world more than any others of that address were the following: "Let every nation know, whether it wishes us well or ill, that we shall pay any price, bear any burden, meet any hardship, support any friend, oppose any foe, in order to insure the survival and success of liberty."

Jim Kotrc fully agreed with that policy and wanted to be a part of it. After all, that's why he went to West Point. He desperately wanted to serve his country and support its friends. He later did so with honor but paid the ultimate price as he became the twentieth fallen warrior of the class on 29 July 1969.

Jim was a hard worker and a true patriot. He was born just outside of Omaha, Nebraska, on 7 June 1940. His older brother, Ron, was two years old at the time. It wasn't long before his father went off to the Second World War. When he returned a few years later he decided to stay in the army. He was proud to have been part of the allied victory and wanted to continue wearing the uniform of a career noncommissioned officer. From 1945 to 1950 the Kotrc family lived on army posts in Arizona and San Francisco. But tragedy struck in 1950 as Jim's dad died at only thirty-nine years of age. So, Mrs. Kotrc and her two sons returned to their roots in Omaha and Jim again became a Nebraskan. He missed his dad and the military way of life, though, and the following year, while in the sixth grade, he announced to his teacher that he wanted to go to West Point. From that moment on Jim never changed his mind as he focused on his goal with increasing intensity. He studied hard, worked hard, and trained hard. For six straight summers he was a low-level employee of the Peony Park Swimming Pool in Omaha. But his diligence eventually paid off and he was elevated to assistant manager his last summer of employment.

At Omaha South High School Jim was a well-known student leader who was highly respected by students and teachers alike. He attained the rank of cadet colonel and commanded the ROTC battalion. He was also the commander of the "Crack Squad" drill team as well as a member of the rifle team. In addition, Jim participated in Boys State, was an Order of DeMolay representative, the president of the Latin Club and a member of the National Honor Society. His high school grades were excellent, but like many of his future classmates, his college board scores were not high enough to secure an appointment to the academy after he graduated in 1958. After all, only one of every ten applicants made it into West Point. So, Jim entered the University of Omaha with the intention of applying for the academy again the following year. However, he was again denied admittance. Instead of giving up, though, Jim became more determined than ever and decided to spend some of his hard-earned money on a prep school that would concentrate heavily on college board preparation. He knew what he wanted and would do whatever it took to achieve his goal. Jim already knew more about West Point than most aspirants since he read everything pertinent he could get his hands on. He knew that it was founded in 1802 with the purpose of providing the nation with leaders of character who would serve the common defense and he knew that during the Revolutionary War a massive iron chain was stretched across the Hudson from West Point to Constitution Island to prevent enemy passage. He knew all about the "Long Gray Line" and wanted to be part of it.

The Colombian Prep School in Washington, D.C., was where Jim went the following year in order to benefit from its emphasis on college board preparation. The move paid off for Jim and it wasn't long before he was a new cadet and a member of the Class of '64.

After such a struggle to get into the academy, Jim wasn't about to complain about the difficulties of cadet life. His ROTC and athletic experience proved to be of great help with the military and physical challenges he encountered. The toughest physical task Jim and his classmates had to face was RECONDO Week, a grueling six days in the field during the summer of 1961 at Camp Buckner. There was little food (some of which was World War II C rations), hardly any sleep (some people got none), and lots of patrolling, land navigation, survival training, and hand-to-hand combat. Any mistakes made

164

in the hand-to-hand combat pit were punished with a trip to the "red rock," where the cadet would do pushups with his feet elevated (on top of the rock painted red). Although Jim's arms were already well developed from a season of gymnastics, they became even more so after numerous visits to the "red rock."

Despite the primitive conditions, fatigue, and lack of time, every cadet was expected to maintain a clean rifle at all times—just as it would be in a combat situation. During one of the frequent rifle inspections, the officer inspector was displeased with the weapon of one of Jim's classmates and decked him with a vertical butt stroke. It was another one of the many tough lessons learned during RECONDO Week.

As a plebe, Jim was a member of the gymnastics team and later became the team manager. He also developed a love of mountaineering and served as the training officer of that club. Perhaps his most unique talent was as an artist. Besides being a member of the Art Club, he did a lot of drawing for cadet publications and friends. One of the beneficiaries of Jim's efforts was Sig Weiner who recalls: "Jim and I were together in Company D-2 during plebe and yearling years. Even though he was a couple of years older than most of us, he had a 'baby face.' He was as nice a guy as you would ever want to meet—he had no enemies. Jim was always happy to decorate things for his friends. I specifically recall his doing three items for me—some lettering on the back of my B-robe (bathrobe), some K-det characters on a pair of cadet pajamas (which I sent to my then girlfriend as a gift), and a cartoon character on the thick brown paper which I used to cover the lift-out tray in my large wooden packing box. Jim wouldn't turn anyone down. He graciously consented to all requests."

Jim's only difficulties as a cadet were in the academic area—some of the courses were killers (calculus, differential equations, electrical engineering, mechanics of fluids, thermodynamics, mechanics of solids, etc.). One of the toughies during cow year was economics and after the first grading session Jim found himself in the last section (besides being graded every day in every class, cadets were placed in sections according to their standing in the course). Fortunately, though, he and his classmates down there were saved by an instructor who was unique in his approach to making sure his students understood what was important. Practically all the professors at West Point, who were mostly captains and majors, were super. They were young and energetic, model officers who were outstanding examples for their students. But Captain Bell, the last section economics instructor, went out of his way with gyrations, beating on the blackboard, and individual attention—all in an effort to pound the key principles into the collective last section heads. He soon came to be known affectionately as "Ding Dong Bell."

Jim graduated, joined the infantry, attended Airborne and Ranger Schools (after his trip to the Virgin Islands, of course), and was assigned to Fort Benning, the "Home of the Infantry." A little over a year later he met the love of his life, Nancy, on a blind date and three weeks later they were married. Shortly thereafter the newlyweds headed for Fort Bragg where Jim attended the Special Forces Orientation Course prior to his Special Forces assignment in Vietnam. Like Martin Green later did, he worked with the Montagnards and grew to respect them tremendously for their diligence and patriotism. The year flew by and Jim returned to Nancy and Fort Benning where he attended the Infantry Officer Advanced Course after a few months of "snowbirding" (doing a short-term military job before a course starts). By the time he completed the course it was well into 1968 and infantry captains were in great demand during that peak period in Vietnam. So, back he went, this time to the Twenty-fifth Infantry Division where he joined the Second Battalion, Twenty-seventh Infantry as a company commander.

It was shortly after his two classmates, Akos Szekely and Carl Winter, had met their fate while leading their companies in the same division. It was a bad era for the class of '64 in the

Twenty-fifth, for on 29 July 1969 Jim Kotrc was also killed while leading his company to the rescue of a Special Forces unit that had been ambushed. Jim had already been well decorated, but on that day, the last of his life, he earned the Silver Star and the Purple Heart. He was the fifth member of the class to die while serving with the "Tropic Lightning" Division. That represents more deaths for the class than were suffered in any other division. Ironically, only the month before, on 8 June, President Nixon had officially initiated the policy of "Vietnamization," the gradual turnover of the war from the U.S. military to the South Vietnamese Armed Forces and the build-up of South Vietnam's war supplies. But it would be awhile before there would be any significant decrease in the American military participation.

It was yet another sad loss for the Class of '64. Jim had just begun to enjoy the finer things in life after his years of struggle and hard work. He had a wonderful marriage and his army career was blossoming as he had already been selected for a below-the-zone promotion (only about five percent attain such early promotions). Jim was promoted to major posthumously.

His mother, brother, and young wife were grief stricken. How could someone so good die so young? His classmates were also upset as they realized they had been steadily losing their buddies for over three years. How much longer would it continue? Tom Kerns's reaction was typical: "When I heard about Jim I was stunned. I really began to wonder why our class was taking so many big hits, especially my old company, L-2. Was it really worth it? First was Hutch, my best buddy, my soul mate. Then, only a year later it was KB, one of the best soldiers any army could ever have. Jim Kotrc was the third '64 victim from our cow and firstie group in L-2. That represents one-eighth of our class in the company! The real tragedy was that all three of them were great guys—dedicated soldiers and real patriots. Jim was a tremendous person, and so strong for his size. I always enjoyed watching gymnastics and remember marveling at what he could do on the high bar. And, I respected him for staying with the team as the manager after he lost his place as a performer. Jim was always a team player, both as a cadet and as an army officer. His was another devastating loss for us."

Jim Kotrc was a giver. He gave all he had for his country, his family, his classmates, and his fellow man. He was laid to rest in the Fort Benning National Cemetery.

Chapter Twenty-one

Robert James Walters

Although he slipped from stardom after his debut at West Point, Bob always seemed to maintain academic prowess over us "goats." Being an upper section mainstay seemed to require little effort, for much of his interest and work was devoted to the Honor Committee and many other non-academic functions. True in his efforts and stubborn in his ideals, Bob will indeed be a credit to the officer corps.

By June of 1970 almost eleven months had passed since Jim Kotrc's death and the U.S. troop strength had been reduced to approximately 380,000. The men of the Class of '64 were feeling a bit better and hoping that no more casualties would be suffered during the remainder of the American involvement in Vietnam. Those hopes were dashed, however, on 27 June when Bob Walters perished. To make matters worse, Alex Hottell (Chapter 22) would meet his fate only ten days later.

Robert James Walters probably had more army blood than anyone in the class, as well as more family ties to West Point. His maternal grandfather, Class of 1908, was the oldest survivor of the Bataan Death March. Bob's father, Paul, was graduated in 1933 and his brother Jim is a member of the Class of 1959. Two uncles were also West Pointers. This unique and patriotic family has proudly combined 133 years of service to country.

Bob's life began on 18 August 1941 in Santa Monica, California, where he joined his parents, Betty and Paul, and his older brother, Jim. At the time, his father was a student at UCLA, working on a masters degree in physics. For the next eighteen years Bob lived the typical, nomadic existence of an army brat. The Walters family continued to grow as Michael arrived four years after Bob and Elizabeth another four years later. After attending schools all around the country, Bob graduated from Francis Hammond High School in Alexandria, Virginia, in 1959. He had been an honor student, Eagle Scout, and sports editor of the yearbook. His main interest was in science, and were it not for the family's traditional heritage of attending West Point, he might have been a scientist. The only problem in continuing that tradition was that

170

academy appointments were hard to obtain in 1959, so Bob enrolled in Sullivan's Prep School in Washington, D.C., and crammed for West Point. Of course he didn't realize at the time that Jim Kotrc was doing the same thing nearby at the Colombian Prep School. The effort also paid off for Bob the following year as he won a presidential appointment, which is probably the most competitive route of all into the academy.

While at West Point, to quote one of his classmates, "Bob was true in his efforts and stubborn in his ideals." He excelled academically, earning stars plebe year, and later graduated number sixty-five in the class. Bob was an exceptionally well-rounded cadet and participated in numerous extracurricular activities such as the Honor Committee, the Debate Council and Forum, the Lacrosse Team, SCUSA, the Cadet Chapel Choir, and the Russian Club. And, as has been mentioned previously, he was one of the five Parachute Club members in the class who would die in Vietnam. During the summer of 1963, Bob gave up his vacation in order to represent West Point with two other cadets on Operation Crossroads. This was a Peace Corps type program in which seventy-two American colleges and universities participated throughout Africa.

Bob was in Ethiopia where he worked with the people on simple but useful projects such as flood control, sanitation, and the construction and repair of roads, school facilities, libraries, and dispensaries. Near the close of his first-class year he wrote the commandant of the Coast Guard Academy requesting permission to join the annual training cruise on their tall ship, *Eagle*. Permission was granted, so Bob and his classmate Pete Danylchuk joined the crew of the *Eagle* after graduation, once again sacrificing leave time! Two months later Bob reported for Ranger and Airborne training at Fort Benning as a second lieutenant of the Corps of Engineers. Shortly thereafter he joined the 173d Airborne Brigade in Okinawa, along with several other classmates, including Jack

Grubbs, who wrote, "We served almost four years together on Okinawa and in Vietnam with the 173d Airborne Brigade and later with the Eighty-second Airborne Division at Fort Bragg. ... Bob gave outstanding combat engineer support to the Second Battalion, 503d Infantry, in Okinawa. ... In May, 1965, the 173d was deployed to Vietnam as the first U.S. Army combat unit to enter the war. Bob was given the mission of preparing the company perimeter for the arrival of the remainder of the company. Being in the advance party, he held the 'dubious' honor of being one of the first, if not the first, of our class to arrive in Vietnam. Throughout his tour he rendered outstanding combat engineer support to the entire brigade, including demolition and mine-clearing missions, building fortifications, and construction of the brigade base camp. An example of his performance was summed up in the commander's combat notes on brigade operations in the famous 'Iron Triangle': 'The engineers had the mission of running the water point just outside the brigade perimeter. Although harassed on four separate occasions by VC rifle fire, grenades, and mortars, this group under Lieutenant Walters continued to function both day and night without complaint or requests for assistance. A job well done.' On numerous occasions Bob's platoon was reorganized as infantry and he led his men into War Zone D, the Plain of Reeds and Ho Bo Woods."

On one such action his platoon made an airmobile assault to secure a landing zone, for which Bob was awarded the Combat Infantryman's Badge. Throughout his one-year tour, the 173d achieved success after success and Bob's engineer troops played a key role. In early 1966 the brigade launched a swift operation into the Mekong Delta, the first time U.S. Army troops set foot in that area. The only difficulty Bob encountered during his year of combat was the harsh reality of losing comrades in arms. The deaths of Clair Thurston and David Ugland during Operation Hump hit him very hard.

In May 1966 Bob returned from Vietnam and was assigned to the Eighty-second Airborne Division's 307th Engineer Battalion. While there he qualified as a jumpmaster and
was awarded the Senior Parachutist Badge. After a year and
a half of Stateside duty, Bob felt the need to broaden his hori-
zons and in February 1968 he volunteered for Special Forces
duty and joined the First Special Forces Group in Okinawa
from where he frequently deployed to Korea and Taiwan. On
one temporary duty assignment to Korea, he was awarded
the Joint Service Commendation Medal for his outstanding
service as the deputy chief of staff, Operations, for the Eighth
Army Engineer, Major General John B. Dillard. Later, in a
letter to Bob, General Dillard wrote, "You may be interested
to know that the entire program (that you) planned is under
contract at just over $100 million and somewhere in the neigh-
borhood of $55 million has actually been placed. We are at
top momentum on the program and I am sure Korea will never
be the same again. ... I hope when you jump from the iron
birds in the sky that you remember to pull the rip cord, but
more importantly, don't jump without that chute. Take care
of yourself. Sincerely, Dillard." (General Dillard was killed
in Vietnam in 1970 when his helicopter was shot down.)

Professional dedication led Bob to volunteer for return
to Vietnam, and in August 1969 he became company commander of the Eighty-seventh Engineer Company of the 199th
Light Infantry Brigade. During his tenure the company won
the Itschner Award, which is awarded annually by the Society of American Military Engineers to the most outstanding
engineer company in the army. The accompanying citation
commended the unit for "...providing unexcelled combat support to deployed elements of the 199th in ever-changing situations. The engineer company often performed missions com-
parable in magnitude to those of an engineer battalion. Its
outstanding effectiveness in bunker destruction and
minesweeping operations contributed significantly to the success of the brigade's combat operations and is indicative of

173

the excellence and esprit de corps of its officers and enlisted men."

Following his six months of company command (the allotted amount at the time) Bob returned to Special Forces duty as the staff engineer of the Fifth Special Forces Group. In that capacity he planned and supervised construction activities for the various elements of the group throughout South Vietnam. Within a week of his departure, while Bob was escorting his replacement around in the group aircraft visiting the various engineer projects, the plane crashed while attempting to land at Dak Ket in the Kontum Highlands area, killing all on board. At first it appeared that the plane had overshot the runway. Later, Bob's classmate Barry McCaffrey looked into the incident and concluded that the landing probably was frustrated by enemy ground fire (a common greeting in such hostile areas), thus causing the failure of the attempted aborted landing. This opinion was shared by Bob's father who was concerned and checked out every possible angle. The bottom line, unfortunately, is that the deaths of Captain Bob Walters and several other dedicated soldiers on 27 June 1970 was another tragic loss for our country and the free world. In addition to the awards already mentioned, Bob had also earned several other medals and citations, to include three Bronze Stars and the Air Medal. Among his effects was a 24 January 1970 note of appreciation from Brigadier General W. R. Bond, the commander of the 199th Infantry Brigade, who had been killed in action on 1 April 1970. How uncanny that Bob and two of the three general officers he had recently worked for were casualties within a few months of each other!

Bob Walters was a man for all seasons—highly intelligent, personable, motivated, and patriotic. He was also sincere and deeply religious. In fact, he was the first lay reader licensed in the Episcopal Church in Okinawa. His death was not only a blow to his family but also to his many friends and classmates. Some of their comments are as follows:

174

Mike Willingham, former high school classmate: "Intangible factors that make me look at whatever I do with a more honest eye and perhaps work harder, hopefully a bit better because of Bob—he had an honest eye and liked hard work. So it is that he is in all people he knew and loved and even in those who will never be able to explain it to you. It is kind of like having him near, looking over my shoulder and helping me along. So, his loss I feel, but the pleasure of knowing him and perhaps of keeping part of his spark alive, that will never leave me."

Pete Elson, West Point classmate: "Bob's strong character and magnetic personality gives us all strength to carry on as he would want us to do. Our getting together at various places always raised my spirits. On his last R&R we enjoyed talking about old times and mutual experiences at the Point, Ranger, and Jump Schools. Bob's 'all the way - airborne' spirit was always present in his speech and manner. We rededicated ourselves to serve to the best of our abilities as long as possible. For Bob's sake, I will continue to do just that."

Jack Grubbs, once again: "Throughout all the time we served together, Bob was a wonderful and true friend. He visited with us often. To my children, a visit from 'Uncle Bob' was a big event at our house. Our comradeship, from the serious moments in Vietnam to the enjoyable capers in the States, will always be a cherished memory."

Bob was a man, a soldier, and a devoted son with warmest concern for his family and a host of friends. Nothing was too remote nor too difficult; his response was always a conscientious effort in the true spirit of willingness to help. We would be remiss to merely say, "Thank you, Bob, well done, good and faithful son." Somehow, by the grace of God, we must be worthy of the freedom and the way of life he fought and died for.

Bob Walters is buried in Arlington National Cemetery, two grave sites away from another warrior and hero, Audie Murphy.

Chapter Twenty-two

John Alexander Hottell III

The rare, raw qualities of athletic prowess and brilliance, which seemed to be a congenital characteristic of Alex, required only the catalyst of maturity to catapult him to success. An incessant source of wonder to his less gifted contemporaries, the hallmark of this man of Napoleonic stature is his incisive intellect, his individuality and his unsurpassable tenacity.

Each and every American death in Vietnam was a tragedy in its own right. If there were a way to classify some as more tragic than others, Alex Hottell's loss would probably be at or near the top of the list. His short, twenty-seven-year life was a series of successes that indicated a potential that would have propelled him to the top level in any walk of life. In Alex's case, it was the army, to which he was totally committed. His short-term plan was to return from Vietnam and teach in the Department of Social Sciences at West Point. In the long term, he undoubtedly would have been one of the army's key leaders. In the words of his classmate and good friend, Waldo Freeman (At the time of this writing, Major General Freeman is the U.S. Army commander in Japan.), Alex "had all the marks of a senior general officer."

John Alexander Hottell III was born in Louisville, Kentucky, on Christmas Eve, 1942, the son of John II, a career army officer, and his wife, Helen. Like Clair Thurston, Bob Serio, and Akos Szekely, Alex was an only child who was always a source of pride and joy for his parents. And, like the other army brats in the class, he attended schools in various corners of the world. As a youngster Alex enjoyed the army life and what it had to offer in the way of educational, patriotic, and leadership opportunities, so it was no surprise that he chose to attend West Point.

As a cadet, Alex quickly earned the respect of all. In the area of brilliance, he had no academic weaknesses and ended up graduating tenth in the class. He would later become a Rhodes Scholar.

In the area of athletics and activities, his extensive extracurricular involvements from being the swimming team's diver to the German Club's program chairman is solid testimony of how well rounded and multitalented Alex was.

Waldo Freeman provides additional details: "I knew Alex in Company E-2 plebe and yearling years. We were both in many of the same sections including advanced German. (His German was excellent.) He was always in or near the section leader's seat. We both came from army families and also had that in common. ... He was well liked and respected despite his excess of brains, talent, athletic ability, and ambition over most of the rest of us. More than most, he knew where he wanted to go and he had a plan to get himself there. For example, about early yearling year he started talking about Rhodes Scholarships. ... Alex worked hard at self-improvement. He also played the guitar and was good at singing popular songs.

"During the '63 summer we were in Germany on the same cycle of AOT. Afterward, he, Cal Kluess, and I bicycled from Frankfurt up the Rhine River to Cologne, staying in youth hostels. We went by train to Hamburg and then bicycled through Lubeck and Travemunde to Copenhagen and even into Sweden. It was a great trip as we tried hard to savor Europe and our brief freedom. Alex had his guitar and entertained all the fellow student travelers (especially females) at the hostels."

It is not often that college students become good friends of their professors, but Alex's intellectual capacity impressed all of his instructors. One of those was Colonel Roger Nye, who would later become deputy head of the History Department. Roger reflects on Alex: "Alex caught my attention in a European History course I was teaching to yearlings. He volunteered that the history textbook carried a quotation from Karl Marx's *Das Kapital* that was not correctly translated from the German. Our German language faculty confirmed his observation. ...

"In subsequent conversation he revealed his discontent with the pace of his learning, and he suggested we create a special seminar. Our first meeting of SIRS (Seminar for Individual Responsibility in Scholarship) was in January, 1962. The one requirement was writing 1,000 words a week into a journal, which would become the basis for seminar discussion on history, philosophy, and military professionalism.

"A month later my 1946 classmate from West Point, the Nicaraguan dictator, 'Tacho' Somoza, came to town and the seven members of SIRS came to my quarters to probe his mind. When Alex had the guts to ask why the Somozas continued to run Nicaragua while the Trujillos had been overthrown in the Dominican Republic, 'Tacho' gave him a one-sided answer. Alex included a four-page summary of that evening in his journal, suspicious but unabashed that 'Tacho' had charmed him.

"As we grew out of SIRS, Al continued to make almost daily journal entries. The journals focused on all aspects of his cadet life but the overriding theme was preparing to continue his post-academy education as a Rhodes Scholar at Oxford. By the time of his death in 1970, the journals had grown to ten bulging three-ring notebooks of typed and handwritten manuscripts."

Alex's widow, Linda, sent the journals to Roger Nye in 1995 for incorporation into the West Point Library's Special Collections. Some of the countless topics discussed in them are as follows: "The duty of man is to fulfill his own nature," "Why officers should be honest," "What is our responsibility in Vietnam?" "We must remain active in developing areas for economic reasons," "What did I learn from West Point?" and "When do I get married?"

Thus Al's journals record a young man's struggle to find intellectual and spiritual guidance for meaningful leadership in the U.S. Army during the chaotic decade of the sixties. Despite the expressed criticisms and uncertainties, Linda has noted that, in his life, Alex was driven by the idea that "You can if you think you can."

In December of firstie year, Al suffered "the worst defeat of my life" when he was turned down for the Rhodes scholarship. That momentary failure motivated him to work harder and reapply the following year. So, Alex spent his two months of graduation leave sharing a dumpy apartment in Greenwich Village with Martin Green and Mike Leonard while attending the New School for Social Research.

After Airborne and Ranger Schools, Alex reported to the 101st Airborne Division at Fort Campbell. Shortly thereafter he passed his Rhodes interviews and was granted the scholarship. Alex's stay at Fort Campbell, although brief, was most significant, for it was there that he met two people who became paramount in his life—fellow second lieutenant, Mike Sierra, and his future wife, Linda Brown. Mike recalls those days and subsequent times: "Alex and I were friends. We met at Fort Campbell in 1964 and I was at his funeral in 1970. During those six years we tried to solve most of the world's problems. At least I tried to help. It was quite clear to me from the outset that Alex had an agenda that was intended to solve most of the world's problems—only he was going to begin with something simple, like the U.S. Army.

"I was always impressed with Alex. He was poised and confident, and he had a swagger about him that could be terribly offensive to some people. I wasn't offended though; I was eager to be part of that whole scene. After all, we were the 101st Airborne Division. Only the best, we were told, were assigned to this elite unit. And we all believed it.

"Alex arrived at Fort Campbell well prepared to begin a long career of dedicated service. He had studied the great battles and reviewed the lessons of enlightened leadership. Now, after what seemed like entirely too many years of preparation, Alex was ready to make his place in the annals of our history. He had so many things to accomplish, so much to do. Alex couldn't waste time and had little of it for people who did not share a vision of what was possible for our army. You see, Alex was filled with a great deal of zeal and enthusiasm, fed by a characteristic sometimes lost all too soon in our lives—idealism. He was an idealist, an idealist with a vision who

180

challenged all he came in contact with. It was his sword but also his anvil. Perhaps time would have caused one to overcome the other. For the moment, he questioned all that his assessment deemed not to fit the model of what was possible for the army that he and his peers would inherit. This included senior officers mired in World War II doctrine and self-aggrandizement; NCO's with a disdain for the new leadership of a more prepared junior officer; peers with less than a full commitment to what was possible. But Alex was not alone. He was part of a distinct group of many such young, proud idealists who wanted to make a difference.

"As such, many people meeting Alex for the first time would fit into one of two groups—those who liked him and those who did not. Like everything else in his life, there was no middle ground. Alex sought and seized the moral high ground. His intellect would be cause for discomfort among the unprepared and for applause from the many who shared his view. This aside, few of his contemporaries who agreed with him shared the same willingness to project their views as vocally as Alex did.

"It was in that context that we met and began our friendship. Alex was fresh from West Point, filled with the pride and professionalism that institution imbues in its graduates. I was a Distinguished Military Graduate from the Infantry Officer's Candidate School at Fort Benning. In my mind, I was as good as Alex and possessed the experience he was still seeking. His poise and confidence only fed mine and provided a special energy between us. Alex had great ideas and opinions on everything and everyone. We began a sharing of those ideas and views that lasted until his death. Over the next six years I was fortunate to be with Alex at Fort Campbell, in Europe, in Vietnam, at Fort Knox, and finally, in a chapel at West Point to listen to his words describing his life and death. If he were not able to talk, he wrote letters, long powerful letters.

181

"Alex had arrived at Fort Campbell unattached. After getting to know him, my then future wife, Kaye, linked him to her charming and witty friend, Linda, from Clarksville, Tennessee. 'Perfect,' Kaye said, 'Just what he needs.' One of their first dates was to a skating rink where Alex, as was his wont to do, proceeded to instruct Linda on the finer skills of skating. Alex was an excellent athlete, and though skating was not his forte, he thought he could certainly go around a rink and impress a southern gal. Linda watched and listened to Alex as he went over the basic routines. Finally, she smoothly skated a choreographed sequence of moves, spins, and turns, finishing with double jumps and the applause of a gathered audience. Kaye turned to Alex and whispered that Linda had been a state champion. 'Why didn't you tell me?' asked Alex as Linda approached. 'Because you never asked,' replied Linda.

"Kaye and I got married in the spring of 1965. Alex and Linda were in our wedding as I prepared to leave a few weeks later, full of excitement and great expectations for my new venture in Southeast Asia. Alex departed for Oxford that fall and we timed our arrival back to Fort Campbell in 1966 so that Kaye and I could be in their wedding. Kaye was a bridesmaid and I was the head usher. Colonel Hottell was the best man. What a wonderful sight—the proud colonel and his gracious wife, beaming at the marriage of their only child, who was their life."

Linda joined Alex after their wedding and the happy couple spent their free time exploring Europe in "Melvin the Mustang." On one trip Linda stayed with Kaye and Mike in Bad Toelz, Germany, while Al spent a week at the German Army Airborne School earning his German jumpmaster qualification. Jumpmaster School is tough enough in English, so Al's German really had to be good. The two couples often traveled together, guided by *Europe On $5 A Day*.

Oxford was an adventuresome three years for Alex and his reaction was stated again and again in just four words: "I love it here." In addition to satisfying the academic demands, he wrote poetry, played guitar in a local combo, "The Turn of the Pooh," and continued adding to his journals, which he admitted had become "...an integral part of my personality. I can't have an interesting experience or stimulating thought without an accompanying compulsion to put it down." Some of the journal entries he made during that time were: "We are doing well in Vietnam; my country, right or wrong," "...our job in Vietnam may take ten years," "If I do not believe in eternal life, how can I send soldiers to their death?" Halfway through the program, some of the other Rhodes Scholars wrote a letter to President Johnson, urging settlement through negotiations in Vietnam. Alex opposed the letter, maintaining that those who were military should not give aid and comfort to the enemy. Along with several other U.S. military scholars at Oxford, Alex began to project a vision for the army that would serve it well into the twenty-first century. Once again, he was the idealist with a vision and he preached it to anyone who would listen and to many who wouldn't.

Toward the end of his sojourn in England, he began focusing on his own future possibilities as he knew he would soon be participating in his country's increasing effort in Southeast Asia. A journal entry discussed his possible demise: "...it is precisely because life is so precious to me that I am prepared to die, and there is no paradox in this. The meaning I found in life is embodied in West Point; not just the place or the people, or even my four years there, but the total concept of the place. Its history reeks of nobility, its sons personify duty and honor, and that other great source of meaning, our country. It is the poetic words of MacArthur, gloom period, football weekends, 'Ladies and Gentlemen, the United States Corps of Cadets.' It is the pride in wearing your country's uniform and giving the troops something to believe in; it is the embodiment of the history of the American fighting man and, by damn, if I die taking part in that, I die happy and satisfied. Of the possible meanings of death, it is the best."

Alex successfully completed his study requirements in July 1968 and was sent to Fort Bragg for some army "re-greening" before going to the combat zone. (He had hoped to go directly to Vietnam with Mike Sierra but the higher-ups said he had been away from troops too long.) For nine months he commanded "The Cobras," Company C, Third Battalion, 504th Infantry of the Eighty-second Airborne Division. He and his troops developed a mutual admiration society and the company was transformed from an also-ran into a top-notch unit of team players. "Captain Cobra" was ready to go to Vietnam. Mike helped get him assigned to the First Air Cavalry Division where Al's clear and directed vision would fit in perfectly with the division's revolutionary concept.

A week before leaving Linda, Alex learned that he was to become a father and pondered the coming sadness over not being able to be with her at her due time. That concern was added to the other normal pre-combat uncertainties.

In the First Cav Alex took over B Company, First Battalion, Eighth Cavalry, the "Pigirons," a unit of mostly draftees. His first reaction was, "By God, they're all CIVILIANS!" But, it didn't take long for him to realize that they were fine, young, red-blooded Americans who were also answering their country's call. He wrote, "People know what they should do and they have the courage and confidence in each other to do it. ... They will do anything even though they feel that life and society have dumped all over them; they can still drive on and fight like demons, march like Jackson, and soldier like the very dickens when they have to...it fills me with inspiration. They are truly the great people of this war...the forgotten civilians who will probably never receive their due for their valor on the fields of battle." The company flourished and on one of its numerous successful operations Alex won the Silver Star for leading his company in a counter-attack rescue of a friendly ambushed unit. In addition to freeing the beleaguered unit, he personally carried three wounded men through heavy fire to the rear. The only low point of Alex's command tour came when he received a letter from Linda stating that she had had a miscarriage.

In the meantime, Mike Sierra returned from Vietnam to the Armor Advanced Course at Fort Knox. "Alex wrote frequently. Whenever his unit enjoyed a pause in the day, he would write. How did he find the time? He had so much to say—on tactics and logistics, on the merits of employing leapfrogging artillery batteries with sweeping infantry platoon units, on the folly of a rotational policy that caused everyone to relearn valuable lessons gained with the lives of soldiers, on the value of strategic bombing and the need to use military power far more wisely than our leaders realized. He wanted to share this vision and I soon realized that he was not selecting just me to share this with. He was reaching out to as many people as would listen. He wanted to make a difference."

The division commander cut short Al's company command tour after four months and made him the division historian so that he could write about the effectiveness of the air cavalry. That mission accomplished, he then was assigned as a G-2 (Intelligence) Operations desk officer on the division staff. By that time he had become so well respected that Major General George Casey, then the assistant division commander, asked Alex to be his aide when he took over the division in June 1970. Of course that meant Alex would have to extend his tour for at least six months, which he did. He went home for a month's leave, visited his parents and friends with Linda, and continued to demonstrate idealism, fire, and passion for his work. At one point he called Mike Sierra aside to tell him of a letter he had left with Linda, to be opened only if "something" happens.

Alex returned to begin his new job in late April and by July the monsoon rains had arrived. On the evening of Saturday, the sixth, Al and his classmates in the division area, Jed Brown (who had been in Linda and Al's wedding four years before) and Jim Carson (a former roommate who was also at

185

Fort Campbell with Al) decided to have a beer in the Officers Club tent. After about two hours of chatting, Al invited Jed to accompany General Casey and himself the next morning on their weekly Sunday visit to the division's wounded soldiers at the Cam Ranh Bay hospital. Although Jed's outfit, the Eighth Engineer Battalion, had several soldiers hospitalized, he declined the offer, stating that he'd probably better stay around and help break in his newly arrived battalion commander.

That decision saved Jed's life, for the next morning en route to Cam Ranh Bay the general's helicopter, descending through the clouds to refuel, crashed into the side of a mountain, instantly killing all on board. It was several days before a massive search found the crash site. In the States, Kaye and Mike rushed to Linda's side. Mike recollects: "The funeral at West Point was a 'Who's Who' of our army at the time. It was profound and moving and emotional and fitting. And it was sad. Linda received the American flag and was left with the memories of the too short marriage and the images of what was to be. Colonel and Mrs. Hottell greeted everyone with a smile and a thank you and internalized their grief. Colonel Hottell died a few years later and his wife soon after. Their grief was overwhelming. Alex, you see, was their life."

Countless soldiers, friends, and family members were deeply saddened by this multiple loss. Alex, like his twenty-one classmates who had already fallen, had been doing his best in the service of his country. And, like Jim Kotrc almost a year before, he died after having been selected for advanced promotion and was promoted posthumously to major.

Alex's family established the Major John Alexander Hottell III Memorial Award (a military saber) which is annually presented to the graduating cadet with the highest standing in European History (Until 1987 the award was for the Modern History course.). Until his death, Alex's dad traveled to West Point to present the award each year. While Jed

Brown was assigned to the Department of History in the early seventies he served as his escort officer.

Among the many extraordinary accomplishments of Alex Hottell was the premonitory letter (mentioned above) to his beloved Linda, written in the event of his death in Vietnam, which became part of his obituary and was published in the *New York Times*. He wrote:

> I am writing my own obituary for several reasons, and I hope none of them are too trite. First, I would like to spare my friends, who may happen to read this, the usual clichés about being a good soldier. They were all kind enough to me, and I not enough to them. Second, I would not want to be a party to perpetuation of an image that is harmful and inaccurate: "glory" is the most meaningless of concepts, and I feel that in some cases it is doubly damaging. And thirdly, I am quite simply the last authority on my own death.
>
> I loved the Army: it reared me, it nurtured me, and it gave me the most satisfying years of my life. Thanks to it I have lived an entire lifetime in 26 years. It is only fitting that I should die in its service. We all have but one death to spend, and insofar as it can have any meaning it finds it in the service of comrades-in-arms.
>
> And yet, I deny that I died FOR anything - not my Country, not my Army, not my fellow man, none of these things. I LIVED for these things, and the manner in which I chose to do it involved the very real chance that I would die in the execution of my duties. I knew this, and accepted it, but my love for West Point and the Army was great enough - and the promise that I would someday be able to serve all the

187

ideals that meant anything to me through it was great enough - for me to accept this possibility as a part of a price which must be paid for all things of great value. If there is nothing worth dying for - in this sense - there is nothing worth living for.

The Army let me live in Japan, Germany, and England with experiences in all of these places that others only dream about. I have skied in the Alps, killed a scorpion in my tent camping in Turkey, climbed Mount Fuji, visited the ruins of Athens, Ephesus, and Rome, seen the town of Gordium where another Alexander challenged his destiny, gone to the Opera in Munich, plays in the West End of London, seen the Oxford-Cambridge rugby match, gone for pub crawls through the Cotswolds, seen the night-life in Hamburg, danced to the Rolling Stones, and earned a master's degree in a foreign university. I have known what it is like to be married to a fine and wonderful woman and to love her beyond bearing with the sure knowledge that she loves me; I have commanded a company and been a father, priest, income-tax advisor, confessor, and judge for 200 men at one time; I have played college football and rugby, won the British National Diving Championship two years in a row, boxed for Oxford against Cambridge only to be knocked out in the first round and played handball to distraction - and all of these sports I loved, I learned at West Point. They gave me hours of intense happiness. I have been an exchange student at the German Military Academy, and gone to the German Jumpmaster School, I have made thirty parachute jumps from everything from a bal-

188

loon in England to a jet at Fort Bragg. I have written an article that was published in *Army* magazine, and I have studied philosophy. I have experienced all these things because I was in the Army and because I was an Army brat. The Army is my life, it is such a part of what I was that what happened is the logical outcome of the life I lived. I never knew what it is to fail, I never knew what it is to be too old or too tired to do anything. I lived a full life in the Army, and it has exacted the price. It is only just.

Alex gave back to West Point that which he had found; and to those who knew and loved him, much more. His life encompassed, transcended, and personified not only "Duty and Honor and Country," but also vision and idealism.

Chapter Twenty-three

David LeRoy Ramsay

Dave Ramsay is one of the oldest in years and maturity in the Class of '64. A good athlete, Dave holds 2 Plebe and 1 "A" Squad record in Track. His sharp mind, outgoing personality and friendliness make him one of the most popular men in the Corps. The combination of his personality and maturity make him a "real good man," and destined for success in life.

On 29 May 1984 *The Boston Globe* published an article entitled " 'Nothing in news' when he died, but now a pilot is remembered." The following are key excerpts from that article:

> Captain David L. Ramsay died when his F-4 fighter jet was shot down near Da Nang on August 17, 1970. His was one of two fighter jets sent out at night to destroy a deadly Viet Cong artillery emplacement. To locate the Communist guns, Ramsay flew low at a slow speed, and was caught in their fire. The Air Force recovered his body the next day.
>
> Yesterday, Ramsay was honored appropriately on Memorial Day with the dedication of Capt. David L. Ramsay Square at the corner of Woodrow and Ballou avenues, Dorchester. VFW Post 8772 [Author's comment: The Veterans of Foreign Wars Post was opened under David's name in 1973.], which is named for Ramsay, paraded a color guard and unveiled the marker. ...
>
> Charles Ramsay, the late pilot's uncle, said, "When he died there was nothing in the news. Now he's getting some recognition. He died doing what he wanted to do. Fly planes and be in combat."

Ramsay, born on Christmas Day 1938, was a native Bostonian. He enlisted in the Air Force, his uncle said, to get away from the Roxbury streets.

At West Point, where he is buried, Ramsay helped gain the admission of his younger brother, Robert, who later piloted a B-52 bomber in Vietnam. The Ramsay brothers were the first pair of black brothers to attend West Point.

Ramsay went back to the Air Force, and became a flight instructor at Laredo Air Force Base in 1967. ... By 1970 Ramsay wanted a combat assignment.

"He wanted to see if the maneuvers he taught really worked," said his uncle. "But his commanding officer at Laredo didn't want to lose him. So Dave went to see Brig. Gen. B. O. Davis, who was in Florida. [Author's comment: Benjamin Oliver Davis, Jr., was an African American West Pointer who was also commissioned in the Air Force. He was graduated near the top of his class in 1936. He retired as a lieutenant general in late 1970, so he most probably held that rank when Dave visited him earlier that year.] He got Davis to make a commitment to him, and I guess Davis outranked his commanding officer by a star."

Cynthia Hall, an aunt, recalled a visit by Ramsay shortly before he went to Vietnam in May 1970. He brought his wife and infant daughter to visit his grandmother, Gladys Ramsay, who raised him.

"If I die, I die," he told his relatives. "It's for my country. That's my mission in life."

Charles Ramsay, a Korean War veteran, remembers telling his nephew to be careful.

"Don't worry about me," he said. "I'm full of booklearning."

The Air Force saved for the family a tape recording made by Ramsay the night before his fatal mission.

"He was standing at the end of the tarmac," said the uncle. "He was reminiscing about his family and how he missed everyone."

Yesterday, post commander Alphonzia Courtney read from a rain-soddened book. "These men and women are worthy of far greater recognition than mere words or markers. The sacrifices they made and the deeds they performed shall be written in history and shall remain alive in our memories for generations to come."

Ramsay, the uncle, pulled his hat brim lower and said, "Personally, I don't think Dave's death served much purpose. But he was doing what he wanted. He was all Air Force, God, Country and Family."

That article said a lot about David Ramsay, but there is a lot more to be said about this unique individual, a proud African American and a true patriot.

Dave's life was a series of challenges, all of which he conquered in admirable fashion. To start with, both of his parents died when he was only five years old, and his brother, Bob, only a year of age. As such, the youngsters were raised by their grandmother, Gladys, a strong-willed woman who, despite far-from-ideal conditions, instilled an exceptionally high degree of discipline and determination in her grandsons. Dave's list of accomplishments is solid evidence.

At English High School in Boston Dave began to emerge as a natural leader of many talents. Besides being a key performer in the Glee Club, he was the drum major of the Drum and Bugle Corps and the president of the Music Appreciation Club. He was also designated as the class song writer and took great pride in writing the lyrics for the class song. As an athlete, Dave's long, strong legs took him to the top levels. His cross-country team won the Massachusetts state championship in 1954 and 1955. The 1954 team also won the New England championship. His 1956 track team took the state championship largely due to Dave's placing first in the 1,000-yard indoor event and the 880-yard outdoor event. And, as a further measure of his diligence, during his senior year in high school, Dave also worked part time after school as a machine operator in the accounting department of a local department store.

After graduating from English High in 1956, Dave enlisted in the air force and a few months later was posted to Japan where he remained for over two years. During that time he gained an appreciation of the U.S. Armed Forces while, at the same time, he was able to continue his development as a track star. In addition to participating in numerous regional meets, Dave was also selected to be a member of the U.S. Air Force's mile relay team.

Eventually it became clear to Dave that what he wanted out of life was to serve his country as an air force officer, and more specifically, as a fighter pilot. He reasoned that there was no better way to achieve that goal than to attend the best officer training school in the world—the U.S. Military Academy at West Point. Although the U.S. Air Force Academy had just gotten underway, Dave still figured that West Point was his best bet since it had already provided countless outstanding officers. So, he put in his request to attend the USMA Prep School at Fort Belvoir, Virginia. It was approved, and Dave reported there in the summer of 1959.

Along with KB Kindleberger, another of Dave's classmates at the prep school was Army PFC Dick Chilcoat, who later became the first captain of the Class of '64. Dick remembers Dave and those formative days well: "We entered the Prep

School in July with over 300 cadet candidates. Eventually, about 180 of us qualified for admission to one of the academies, ninety or so went on to West Point, and forty-four graduated four years later with the Class of '64.

"Dave Ramsay was the only black cadet candidate in our Prep School class, and was one of only two (Warren Miller was our other black classmate) in our West Point class. By setting standards of excellence that were worthy of emulation by all of us, Dave paved the way for future generations of black cadets and established a legacy that would sustain them at West Point and, ultimately, in their service to our nation.

"In the summer of 1959, I remember early on observing Dave as we stood in the cadet candidate company formations. I was in Third platoon and he was in Second platoon. 'Rams,' as he came to be known, was tall, lean, and ramrod straight. In Air Force Blue, standing rock-solid at attention amongst a sea of Army Green, he exemplified the words, 'military bearing and appearance.'

"As we learned quickly, he was also a man of great intelligence, warm and sincere demeanor, and dignified carriage. Honesty and integrity characterized his every word and deed. His sense of humor, manifested by a wide grin and a glint in the eye, along with his countenance and character...won him many friends and a thousand admirers. He excelled in the classroom, on the drill field, and on the athletic field. In sports, Dave's speed, power, ability, and grace were awesome.

"More than any other attribute, we were impressed with his leadership qualities. He was a standout. A natural leader. Dave was a pacesetter in a platoon of gifted cadet candidates that included soldiers, airmen, marines, and sailors such as Chartrand, Clements, Davis, Gibbs, Grubbs, Gundisson, Higgins, Jackson, Ketton, Kindleberger, McLemore, Mortensen, Moore, Norwell, Sprague, and Wells, to name a few.

"Yes, Dave Ramsay was easy to remember...because he was a standard-bearer of excellence at the USMA Prep School as well as at West Point. He was someone to guide on and destined to make history in our hearts and in our minds. How could he not? Dave was all that we wanted to be: a leader of character."

It was a proud moment for Dave when he shed his air force blue for cadet gray on 5 July 1960. In so doing, he joined the Class of '64 as one of its older and wiser members and with more military experience than anyone else who took the oath that day.

As a cadet, Dave continued to excel as a runner and broke the plebe indoor track record for the 1,000-yard run during his first year. And, he was also a member of the record-breaking plebe two-mile relay team during that same indoor track season. Later, while on the varsity track team, Dave again participated in setting a two-mile relay record in indoor track. Although Akos Szekely concentrated on longer distance running than Dave, the two of them spent a lot of time together on the cinders and developed a great mutual respect. No one at that time could have possibly imagined what their similar fates would be, least of all, their admiring track coach, Carleton Crowell.

One of Dave's greatest thrills in sports and in life occurred during his firstie year when he was joined on the track team by a young yearling, Bob Ramsay. Dave had set such a good example for his younger brother that Bob followed in his footsteps exactly—after high school, he joined the air force, attended the West Point Prep School en route to the academy, and then, after graduation, went back into the air force as an officer and pilot. The only difference was that Bob became a bomber pilot. Bob, why didn't you tell Dave that he should have been a bomber pilot, too?

Within the class, Dave's reputation as a leader was well known to all. In fact, in his Camp Buckner evaluation in 1961 his TAC wrote, "I believe that this man is the most outstanding cadet in his class!" It was no surprise when he was selected to be a company commander during firstie year.

It was also no surprise when Dave chose to return to the air force after graduation. Until the Air Force Academy began providing air force officers several years earlier, West Point had been supplying that service a good number of its officers. By 1964, however, air force slots were limited for USMA grads, and Dave was one of only fifty-four in the class to don the blue.

During the following six years David Ramsay distinguished himself by a solid record of outstanding achievement—after graduation from flight school at the top of his class he became a flight instructor, a job which he undertook with his characteristic zeal and skill. Recognized as one of the best, Dave was repeatedly singled out for honors and positions of greater responsibility.

While his career was on the rise, Dave took time out to marry Elizabeth Yancey in 1966 and on 5 February 1969 their daughter, Nicole, was born. As has been the case with the children of the other fallen warriors of '64, Nicole never had the opportunity to get to know her father and benefit from his upbringing. Dave's grandson, though, Jonathan David, is benefitting from his mother's loving care—as well as that of his doting grandmother.

In Vietnam Dave had been assigned to the Fourth Tactical Fighter Squadron at Da Nang Air Base. He had only been in country for three months when his plane went down, but in that short amount of time, he had been awarded a Silver Star and two Distinguished Flying Crosses along with a handful of other medals. And, he had already been selected for subsequent assignment to the U.S. Air Force Thunderbirds' Aerial Demonstration Team, an honor falling to only a very select few.

Dave's was one of 2,340 U.S. Air Force deaths in Southeast Asia. That represents only four percent of the total of names on the Vietnam Memorial. But the loss of David LeRoy

Ramsay has to be one of the most severe because he was so much for so many. Within the Class of '64, he was one of our most respected leaders and we thought he was indestructible. Within the air force he was a star on the rise, in more ways than one. Within his race he was the epitome of pride and success. And, within his family, he was the ideal son and grandson, the exemplary brother and a most loving and caring husband and father.

When Dave died, the war in Vietnam was still going strong although the number of American military personnel had dropped to less than 400,000. It had been a bad summer for the Class of '64, however, as it lost three of its finest—one each month, and all three aircraft related.

Chapter Twenty-four

John Meigs Graham

John, with a ready smile for everyone, always managed to look at the bright side of life and this bright side always included Nancy. Due to his desire to excel and innate ability to get along with others, he is assured success in whatever he might undertake after graduation. John will long be remembered for "Special Orders #69."

In early 1971, shortly after the death of her husband, Nancy Graham received a letter from the commander of the U.S. Military Assistance Command, Vietnam, General Creighton W. Abrams, which read as follows:

> On behalf of the US Military Assistance Command, Vietnam, I wish to extend my sympathy to you over the loss of your husband, Captain John M. Graham, United States Army, and express my condolences during your time of sorrow and bereavement.
>
> It is my hope that you will find a measure of solace in knowing your husband gave his life for a noble cause, the defense of liberty in the free world. Rest assured that we who remain here in Vietnam will continue our efforts to bring peace to this troubled land so that your husband's sacrifice will not have been in vain.

John Graham was born in Owensboro, Kentucky, on 9 March 1939, the son of Harriet and Miller. He was baptized John, after his paternal grandfather, who was superintendent of schools for Davis County, and Meigs, for the maternal O'Bryan ancestors who served in the Civil War and in the medical profession.

John attended the Charlestown schools after his family moved with the DuPont Corporation to Southern Indiana. Stories of his childhood days revolved around family picnics, Mass on Sundays followed by his mother's fried chicken, fishing trips with his dad and his school buddy, Stanley

Bartholomew, camping with the Boy Scouts, caring for the family horses and pets, and playing the trumpet in Mr. Sawyer's high school concert band.

By the time high school graduation rolled around, John was president of the senior class, guard on the varsity basketball team, first trumpet in the Jonathan Jennings High School Band, which led to a college music scholarship, and, after school, he was the manager of the local auto service station.

As the oldest of eight children, he mourned with his close-knit family when his dad died unexpectedly. John's mother, brother, David, and sisters Virginia, Carolyn, Janet, Marybelle, Marlee, and Mimi all settled back in Owensboro, and John enlisted in the army in June of 1957.

In 1959 he graduated from the USMA Prep School and entered West Point with the Class of 1963. He later joined the Class of '64 after losing a battle with the Math Department. His favorite cadet stories include "swimming to Newburgh," the plebe laughing bag, the five-year academic plan, attaining Century Club status on the area, H-I and G-1 water polo teams and, in 1961, meeting his "Yankee Filly," Nancy Mullin, from Greenwood Lake, New York.

Nancy and John were married three days after graduation and they spent summer leave sailing Cape Cod and the lakes of Kentucky. The next years as an infantry officer were fast paced, exciting, and memorable as a time filled with familial love and joy as new parents, pride in his professional accomplishments, and dedication to Duty. . .Honor. . .Country.

Classmate Mike McKinley became a very close friend of John's and has recalled their times together: "We first got to know each other during Ranger School when we shared the adventures of being on the same patrol several times. I recall taking many "map reconnaissance" breaks together under a poncho with John during rain storms along with about ten other classmates who smoked. It is a marvel our lungs survived those days.

"We really drew close during our first assignment together in Kitzingen, Germany, as the only graduates in the First Battalion, Fifteenth Infantry, commanded by Lieutenant Colonel Frank Phelps Jones, a former professor at West Point and about as fine a commander as any young officer could hope for. Our first six months were a blur, meeting occasionally between ranges at Hohenfels and Wildflecken with our units or supporting "Marne" tank gunnery at Grafenwohr. While John and I braved the cold at the training centers during our first German winter, Nancy, as I reflect, used to drive around Kitzingen with the heat on full blast because our host landlords were not inclined to increase the fuel in the apartment as the temperature dropped.

"John had two chances to excel as a junior officer in our battalion that I did not envy. Once his musical prowess surfaced, he was appointed the battalion bugler at our Monday morning command reveille formations. A good musician is not necessarily at his best at 5:30 A.M. in snow storms with below freezing temperatures, and John was no exception. Despite the occasional "flubs" and the snickering of 700 troops, John maintained both his dignity and sense of humor through it all. His other chance to excel was a command performance each Sunday morning at 7:00 in the gym, boxing and wrestling with his fellow company officers and their commander. Despite the fact that he had to face a collegiate wrestling champ and a first-string linebacker in the ring each week, he did so cheerfully, something I found to be utterly amazing as a young bachelor who was out late on Saturday nights.

"John's door was always open for bachelor friends such as me, in spite of the shoe-string budget of junior officers at the time. Nancy did her best to instill as much civility into me as she could during those days, and used to invite me over to their apartment for some delicious home-cooked meals quite frequently. On one occasion, when John, Jr. was a toddler (he had been born in 1965), she invited both the Catholic chaplain and me over for dinner. While John and Nancy were assembling dinner, John, Jr. (who was allegedly in my care at the time) proceeded to knock religious artifacts off the wall and the table, sending them crashing and breaking on the floor with one swipe of his hand. Nancy, of course, was horrified that her son did this in front of our parish priest, and I was in the dog house for being such a 'Klutz' as a baby-sitter. I told this story to John, Jr., in Grant Hall during our twentieth reunion when he was a cadet.

"The recurring theme throughout my association with John in Kitzingen is that he was the epitome of an officer and a leader of men, a gentleman, husband, and father. No one could know John Graham and fail to appreciate his love of life. He survived some tough experiences in Europe as a commander with the rapid draw down for Vietnam and subsequent rapid buildup of troops. Those were times that tried our mettle almost as much as combat, and John maintained the respect of his superiors, peers, and subordinates, too, which was, indeed, a challenge in that era. During his tour he was a rifle and weapons platoon leader, company executive officer, battalion adjutant, and he also organized and led the Third Infantry Division's 'Can Do' marching team to Nijmegen, Holland, for the annual five-day peace march. He then commanded the first of his three company-level commands, Headquarters and Headquarters Company of the division's Second Brigade. John was my friend, my confidante, my classmate, and the friendship we shared remains one of life's happiest memories."

After the birth of Anne Mary in 1967, John reported to the First Infantry Division in Vietnam. Classmate Karl Robinson, who was in the same battalion, recalls those times: "I didn't know John well at West Point. I really got to know him well during our first tour in Vietnam in 1967-1968 when we both served as company commanders in the 1/18 Infantry. Bill Annan and Watts Caudill were also company CO's in the battalion during that year. Our battalion CO's were LTC (later GEN) Richard Cavazos and LTC George Tronsrue. It was a great battalion that did great things, perhaps as a result of the intersection of inspired leadership with members of the dynamite Class of '64.

"Our area of operations was Military Region III. The battalion headquarters was at Di An, outside of Saigon, but the battalion spent its time on the Bien Hoa, An Loc, Lai Khe, Quan Loi axis with forays into parts of the Iron Triangle and the Elephant's Ear and up as far as Xuan Loc. We always seemed to be called upon when things heated up, such as when the battle of Loc Ninh broke out in late 1967 and we 'rode to the rescue' and found ourselves in several big fights in the week that followed. Likewise, we were on the division perimeter at Lai Khe on the night the Tet offensive began in 1968, and the next day found us conducting 'combat in cities' operations in Saigon. Since the companies were normally scattered about rather than together as a battalion, we company commanders had limited opportunities to spend together, but the time we had was normally genuinely enjoyable as we tried to relax from the daily rigors of continuous combat operations.

"As a result of the personnel assignment system that carefully matches individual needs and capabilities with the army's needs, after Vietnam, John and I were assigned to the Third Civil Affairs Group (Airborne) at Fort Clayton, Panama Canal Zone. It was in this strange and unique unit that our families got to know each other well. We both lived in government quarters in a housing area at the bottom of the hill where Building 519 stood. Building 519 had once been the hospital and still contained medical facilities; but it also housed the Civil Affairs Group. After a year in Vietnam, this was a perfect opportunity to decompress, to undergo physical and mental renewal, and to make up for lost time with our young families.

"The office routine was non-stressful, evenings, weekends, and holidays were free to enjoy relaxed time together, and the beaches and tropical pleasures of Panama were readily available. Our kids were about the same ages and we shared birthday parties and picnics at the beach; John was Santa Claus at Christmas, and when we really got adventurous, we would launch an expedition to somewhere semi-exotic like Taboga Island in the Gulf of Panama.

"Imbued with the enthusiasm of youth, neither one of us could completely resign ourselves to the sedentary nature of the life of a staff officer, so we both volunteered to attend the Jungle Operations Training Course and the Air Force Jungle Survival Course while we were there.

"During the duty days John and I shared the excitement of periodic parachute jumps out of L-19 Bird Dogs and DC-3's, and visits all over Panama coordinating civic action projects. In the course of all that, we shared stories of our childhood, reflections on the state of world affairs, and mused about what the future might bring.

"Perhaps the greatest adventure we shared in Panama was when we were assigned the project of visiting all of the troop units in the Canal Zone to recruit enlisted volunteers to apply to attend West Point. The previous year was the first in memory when vacancies in the incoming class went unfilled due to an absence of qualified applicants. In an attempt to remedy this problem, the army's leadership decreed that the word should go forth on the opportunities offered by enrollment in West Point, and the bushes should be beaten to flush out "volunteers." This was during 1968-1969 when the popularity of the Vietnam War was at an all-time low and the military in general, and the army in particular, were generally held in low regard, especially among the college population. The soldiers of the Canal Zone had either just returned from Vietnam, or would be headed that way shortly. To say that we were confronted with unreceptive audiences would be a dramatic understatement.

"In particular, I recall a trip to Fort Gulick on the Atlantic side of the Canal Zone to give our pitch to an infantry battalion which was in the field for training. About twilight, the battalion's enlisted contingent was herded into an outdoor amphitheater and the NCO's and officers departed the area for a cookout on the beach. The troops had already been drinking and had brought numerous cases of beer to the evening's 'entertainment.' Never had two pigeons been better set up for a challenging evening's work. We started our pitch about dark and, as we proceeded, the cat calls, shouted obscenities, and eventually, empty beer cans that sailed out of the faceless and unruly crowd punctuated what might otherwise have been a fairly straightforward and informative briefing. As time went on, John and I dodged beer cans, talked faster and faster, flipped through slides at a blinding rate, finished our briefing, and ran for our lives. Once we were back in our truck and a safe distance down the road, we both burst into howls of laughter which were generated far more by the relief of having escaped alive than by the humor one could extract from a difficult and rather harrowing experience.

"Our stay in Panama was interrupted after about a year by orders to Fort Benning to attend the advanced course, but, although our peaceful year in Panama was over, our friendship was able to continue as both families moved into Custer Terrace. But that year also sped by far too fast for either of us, because we knew that, when it was over, we were both due back in Vietnam. And, indeed, back we went, he to a MACV assignment in the Delta, and I to the First Cav Division. It was there that I received a letter from my wife saying that she had received a call telling her that John had been killed in action on 16 January 1971. Of all the losses I saw, knew of, or heard of, John's death was the most personal to me. After three years of close friendship, John was gone. He had died as he had lived, doing his best to help others."

Captain John Graham was posthumously awarded his second Silver Star and Purple Heart for his ultimate bravery. He had volunteered to accompany a reaction force which had the mission of rescuing a trapped unit. En route to the unit's location, they encountered a numerically superior, well-dug-in enemy force. In the ensuing battle, John repeatedly exposed

206

himself to hostile fire while leading several attacks against the enemy positions. The trapped unit was saved but John was mortally wounded.

In addition to those decorations John had also been awarded three Bronze Stars (with V), three Air Medals, and several Vietnamese awards. He was buried with full military honors at the West Point cemetery after a Mass of the Resurrection at the Catholic Chapel.

John M. Graham, Jr., graduated from West Point in 1987 and has served with the Tenth Mountain Division, Eighteenth Airborne Corps, and the Nineteenth Support Command in Korea. His sister, Anne Graham Bryer, graduated from Marymount College in 1989 and is a manpower analyst for the army.

Nancy says, "We were and are blessed to have had John as our husband, father, son, brother, nephew, cousin, friend, and classmate. He has a memorial at the Fort Knox Museum, the Vietnam Memorials in Albany, New York; Frankfort, Kentucky; and in our nation's capital. You know, Johnny,...you are always in our hearts with the love and the peace that you cherished. ... God Bless you."

Karl Robinson continues: "John was a man who was ahead of his time when it came to his outlook on life. In his mid-twenties, he had already figured out what most of us didn't realize until we were in our forties, and that was simply that our families were far more important than our careers, or our financial well-being, or the relative importance of our positions. He knew that time not spent with Nancy and the kids was time that was gone forever. His sense of duty to the army and the nation took him away more than he liked, but his sense of perspective ensured that he made the most of every chance he got to be with those he loved. That understanding grew out of a childhood spent in a strong and loving family, a fact made apparent to me as I listened to him talk about his childhood, his parents, and the rest of the relatives he loved and respected for their devotion to each other.

"John's legacy lives on in the lives of those of us who were fortunate enough to know him well, and learn from his example. You do the best you can in life with the gifts and opportunities that are available to you. Life is not all that complicated unless you make it so. Do what is right, treat those around you with kindness and respect, be patient and understanding with those you love, and don't miss a chance to smile, laugh, and enjoy life.

"I am sure that John is bursting with pride for all of his family loved ones. Nancy, who carried on in spite of her loss, and the two wonderful children who continue his example are doing their best to make the world a better place for everyone."

John Graham was the last '64 warrior to die in combat. Well done, John. Be thou at peace.

Epilogue

Why did I take on this project? The seeds were sown during the thirtieth reunion of our class in October 1994. At the memorial service for these fallen warriors and our other classmates who have left this world, I thought to myself, "Here we are, mostly successful and healthy, enjoying this wonderful weekend, and our deceased compatriots have missed out on this and many other opportunities. It's not fair. What could I possibly do to honor them, especially those who died so young, in combat?" Within a few months the idea evolved and I committed myself to put together this anthology. It has been a most rewarding experience. Many have called it a "labor of love." In the process, I have gotten to know many wonderful people—the families, friends, and fellow classmates of this great group of Americans.

Of these twenty-four brave patriots, the several that I knew well were among the finest young men in our class. As I researched their stories, and those of the others whom I did not know so well, it became clear that the entire group was a collection of outstanding individuals, all of whom had unlimited potential for success in the military or any other future endeavor.

One of many interesting observations I learned from my research is that all twenty-three of those in the army won their Ranger Tab without being recycled (being dropped back a class). One hundred percent! That says a lot, considering that the first-time completion rate for Ranger School has historically been around fifty percent. But, probably most sig-

209

nificant about this illustrious group is the compelling desire that each and every one of them had to serve his country. Despite the eventual moot results of the Vietnam conflict, and the political and psychological turmoil that occurred, these young men believed wholeheartedly that what they did was right—they answered their country's call to help a friendly nation try to prevent being taken over by Communism. As far as they knew, they were participating in a victory for the free world. I'm sure none of them imagined that their efforts might be in vain.

They were a mixture of scholars and athletes, country boys and city slickers, army brats and civilians, married and single—but they all shared the attributes of patriotism, mental and physical toughness, and unselfishness. The idea of service before self was ingrained in each of them.

Did these fine young soldiers die in vain? There are those who say, "Yes, we should not have wasted one American life in Vietnam..." And, there are those who say, "No, we fought in pursuit of a most honorable cause...the rest of Southeast Asia was saved...and, now Vietnam is returning to a free-world economy..." This issue has been debated ad infinitum and will continue to be so.

One thing is certain—all of our country's combat casualties in Vietnam and the Dominican Republic created great sadness for their loved ones. Many of their parents were never the same again. Most of the casualties did not receive the recognition or credit they deserved for laying their lives on the line. Some were harassed and spat upon. We, as a nation, can rectify that. It is never too late to honor our fallen heroes.

West Point's Class of 1964 did not have the highest number of casualties among all of the classes that participated in Vietnam—nor was it the most decorated. It was actually quite typical of the other classes from the sixties, but was still unique in its own way. Not many will argue against it being the class most experimented with in recent times.

Today the Class of '64 is doing everything possible to pay homage to its fallen combat heroes. They and their families, who have suffered the most, certainly deserve it. For example, behind Herbert Hall (the Association of Graduates building at West Point) there is a brick patio which contains their names inscribed in twenty-four of the bricks. Before each class reunion, rubbings are made of the twenty-three engraved names of our classmates on the Vietnam Memorial and are brought to the reunion for appropriate recognition. Also, before each reunion, grave sites of all our deceased are visited by classmates in the vicinity.

This book is another attempt to belatedly pay just tribute to these obedient soldiers. The many contributors to this effort have enthusiastically endorsed its theme. The following comment from Doctor John M. Shaner, Charlie Hutchison's hometown pal, although specifically referring to Hutch, is representative of how all the families, friends, and classmates of these twenty-four heroes feel: "... I sure have enjoyed writing. It has given me the opportunity to rekindle an old friendship and spark some great memories. I have never forgotten Hutch, but as I grow older I find that the memories are even sweeter than I had imagined. Do him justice, John, he was a hell of a friend and an even greater young man. Time will pass, and so will we, but your book will see to it that he is not forgotten."

In closing, there is probably no one more appropriate to pen the final lines than the Reverend Sam P. Lamback, Jr., USMA '64, currently the pastor of the Byron United Methodist Church near Macon, Georgia. Sam spent a full thirty-year career in the army, initially as an artillery officer, and later as a chaplain. He had a tour in Vietnam in each capacity. His contribution to our thirtieth reunion memorial service was instrumental in my undertaking of this tribute. Sam has graciously composed the following verses for these Stars of '64 who gave everything for their country:

EPILOGUE

Consider now this calendar of sacrifice and fame,
The twenty-four of sixty-four, each story, face, and name;
Two dozen of the hundreds who set out across the earth,
So early taken from us as new dreams were giving birth.

Before a single year had passed Charles Hutchison was lost,
In the Dominican Republic he paid the highest cost;
Always the towering leader, dependable and true,
He led the class in sacrifice, what we'd expect he'd do.

Clair Thurston's last heroics seemed strangely parallel,
To Hutch's final bravery, both stories proudly tell;
With, "Follow me!" Clair led his men and gave his all that day,
He died as Hutch, though half a year and half a world away.

Then just across the battlefield Dave Ugland fought with pride,
So duty bound, "glad to be here," he risked himself and died;
Next KB Kindleberger fell, a general he'd surely be...
Instead we led his caisson, as MacArthur's was by KB.

'Uncle Denis' Galloway and likable Dee Stone,
Both leaders and musicians whose zest for life has shown
Us all within the 'system' to serve and have some fun,
And though their lives were shortened, our great respect they won.

The profile of the warrior took on a tragic style,
When new Captain Jim Powers died and left his unborn child;
Cliff McKittrick, still our ray of hope, our single MIA,
Upon his sterling memory we shall forever pray.

Dave Bujalski, friendly giant and loyal engineer,
Fell victim to a sniper in the dawn of his career;
Huachuca's fine "Bujalski Field" shows how his life affected
His soldiers, one who states, he was "revered, loved, and respected."

212

"The bravest man I've ever seen," Mike Kiley was his name,
Skydiver, brave Hal Kaufman, both dates of death the same;
A legacy of courage there on Hill 875,
Commends to us such spirit as long as we're alive.

My good friend, Kirby Wilcox, a 'Rabble-rouser' too,
I chuckle at the happy times as I remember you;
And eloquent Bob Serio, leader, athlete, 'hive,'
They died heroes in combat, but within us they survive.

Mike Nawrosky, Akos Szekely, (we're talking 'world class' here!)
The wounded "Jim Thorpe of Dumont," showed us how to perse-
vere;
The pride of his native Hungary, 'Zek,' none better could uphold,
His record of superlatives, like a legend yet untold.

Carl Winter came from Michigan, Bill Black from Tennessee,
Both left young sons to later learn their fathers' legacy;
But 'duty, honor, country' set limits to their years,
Encouraging their loved ones to new life out of our tears.

Gerry Palma's calling to his God and country too,
Led him to lay his life down, such a natural thing to do;
Relieving a beleaguered force he gave his final breath,
"To live a soldier's life," he wrote, "... and die a soldier's death."

"No greater love..." than Martin Green's, who died to save another,
Extended twice with the Montagnards, who regarded him as brother;
Jim Kotrc also served those tribes and later gave his all
For an ambushed Special Forces team while answering their call.

The ironies of life and death, Bob Walters and Hottell,
Aircraft crashes took them, one prophecy to tell;
Bob's early tour in '65, and death among the last,
While Alex's testament nourishes us like an elegant repast.

213

Indeed Dave Ramsay's record soared beyond which few can trace,
The Thunderbird selectee, a credit to his race;
And last of all, John Graham, while on his second tour,
Died in relief of ambushed troops; his service shall endure.

These soldiers, leaders, patriots; these husbands, fathers, friends,
Whom classmates knew more modestly, their legacy transcends;
The politics and strategies leaving challenges in store,
As we dedicate our service to the Warriors of '64.

BIBLIOGRAPHY

Aitken, Jonathan. *Nixon: A Life*. Washington, D.C.: Regnery Publishing, 1993.

Atkinson, Rick. *The Long Gray Line*. Boston: Houghton Mifflin Company, 1989.

Berry, F. Clifton, Jr. *Sky Soldiers*. Toronto, New York, London, Sydney, Auckland: Bantom Books, 1987.

Bourman, John S. *The Vietnam War - An Almanac*. New York: World Almanac Publications, 1985.

Clarke, Jeffrey J. *Advice and Support: The Trial Years, 1965-1973*. Washington, D.C.: U.S. Government Printing Office, 1988.

Just, Ward. "West Point Rendezvous." *Atlantic*. January 1975.

Kahin, George McT. *Intervention*. New York: Alfred A. Knoph, 1986.

Karnow, Stanley. *Vietnam: A History*. New York: The Viking Press, 1983.

Kearns, Doris. *Lyndon Johnson and the American Dream*. New York, Hagerstown, San Francisco, London: Harper and Row, 1976.

215

Maitland, Terrence and McInerney, Peter. *A Contagion of War*. Boston: Boston Publishing, Company, 1983.

Marantz, Steve. " 'Nothing in news' when he died, but now a pilot is remembered." *The Boston Globe*. 29 May 1984.

McNamara, Robert S. *In Retrospect: The Tragedy and Lessons of Vietnam*. New York: Random House, 1995.

Murphy, Edward F. *Dak To*. Novato, CA: Presidio Press, 1993.

Nixon, Richard. *No More Vietnams*. New York: Arbor House, 1985.

Pisor, Robert. *The End of the Line*. New York and London: W. W. Norton and Company, 1982.

Santoli, Al. *Everything We Had: An Oral History of the Vietnam War by Thirty-Three American Soldiers Who Fought in It*. New York: Random House, 1981.

Schwarzkopf, H. Norman. *It Doesn't Take a Hero*. New York, Toronto, London, Sydney, Auckland: Bantom Books, 1992.

Stanton, Shelby L. *Vietnam Order of Battle*. Washington, D.C.: US News Books, 1982.

Summers, Harry G., Jr. *On Strategy: A Critical Analysis of the Vietnam War*. New York: Dell, 1984.

Summers, Harry G., Jr. *Vietnam War Almanac*. New York, Oxford: Facts On File Publications, 1985.

Westmoreland, William C. *A Soldier Reports*. New York: Doubleday, 1976.

ABOUT THE AUTHOR

Fallen Warriors, The West Point Class of 1964 is John F. Murray's first book, a tribute to his classmates from West Point. Murray, a retired colonel who served in Vietnam, Korea, Europe, and Latin America, is currently a adjunct professor of Spanish at George Mason University and Northern Virginia Community College in Northern Virginia.